The Skills-Powered Organization

The Journey to the Next-Generation Enterprise

Ravin Jesuthasan and Tanuj Kapilashrami

The MIT Press
Cambridge, Massachusetts
London, England

The MIT Press would like to thank the anonymous peer reviewers who provided comments on drafts of this book. The generous work of academic experts is essential for establishing the authority and quality of our publications. We acknowledge with gratitude the contributions of these otherwise uncredited readers.

This book was set in ITC Stone Serif Std and ITC Stone Sans Std by New Best-set Typesetters Ltd. Printed and bound in the United States of America.

Library of Congress Cataloging-in-Publication Data

Names: Jesuthasan, Ravin, 1968- author. | Kapilashrami, Tanuj, author.
Title: The skills-powered organization : the journey to the next-generation
  enterprise / Ravin Jesuthasan and Tanuj Kapilashrami.
Description: Cambridge, Massachusetts : The MIT Press, [2024] | Includes
  bibliographical references and index.
Identifiers: LCCN 2024001000 (print) | LCCN 2024001001 (ebook) |
  ISBN 9780262049238 (hardcover) | ISBN 9780262379809 (epub) |
  ISBN 9780262379816 (pdf)
Subjects: LCSH: Manpower planning. | Vocational qualifications. | Skilled labor. |
  Organizational effectiveness.
Classification: LCC HF5549.5.M3 J47 2024 (print) | LCC HF5549.5.M3 (ebook) |
  DDC 658.3/01—dc23/eng/20240109
LC record available at https://lccn.loc.gov/2024001000
LC ebook record available at https://lccn.loc.gov/2024001001

10 9 8 7 6 5 4 3 2 1

To my children Nadia and Daniel, whose love, curiosity, and openness to new ideas and new people fill me with hope and optimism as to how the next generation of talent will navigate the skills-powered organization.
—Ravin Jesuthasan

To my team at Standard Chartered, who inspire me every day with their passion for reimagining the future of work, my parents for their constant encouragement, and, finally, my "A team"—Abhinav and Ahana—for being my biggest cheerleaders and thought partners.
—Tanuj Kapilashrami

Let the measure of worth not be in the gold amassed, but in the mastery of skills pursued and the breadth of knowledge applied. For in the economy of tomorrow, the true currency shall be the prowess with which one crafts the world—Adapted from an amalgam of wisdoms

Chat GPT 4.0

Contents

Introduction: Becoming a Skills-Powered Organization

We create boxes to make sense of the world. We compartmentalize news, risks, and emotions to process and understand them. We also talk about organizations and jobs as boxes as a means for allocating and structuring work. Employees sit inside jobs that sit inside organizations. This is how we think work gets done. In practice, it's never that cut and dried, but the simple mental model works—or at least it used to.

For the past 140 years, work has primarily been organized around jobs in functional hierarchies as the primary currency of work. This job centricity has been the primary mechanism governing how talent is connected to work, how work is deployed, and how organizations are structured. Jobs have been the currency of the operating system that underpins all organizational infrastructure, from human resources (HR) systems to finance and accounting to enabling technology systems. Now, we are seeing those comfortably familiar boxes begin to disintegrate. This book proposes that accelerated change, demands for organizational agility, artificial intelligence (AI) and work automation, efforts to increase diversity and equity, and emerging alternative work arrangements are rapidly revealing that the traditional work operating system based on jobs and jobholders is too cumbersome and ill-suited to the future. We are seeing the basic building blocks of work erode as jobs give way to skills as the currency of work.

The move to skills as the currency of work is gaining momentum as industry and policymakers deal with some of the most vital talent gaps. As early as 2017, Ginni Rometty, the former CEO of IBM, was an adamant proponent of this approach. Rometty suggested these are "new collar jobs," neither traditionally blue- nor white-collar. In the United States alone, there were more than five hundred thousand open jobs in tech-related sectors in 2022.[1] In a *USA Today* column, Rometty explained that not all tech jobs require a college degree. "At several IBM's locations . . . as many as one-third of employees don't have a four-year degree," Rometty wrote. "What matters most is that these employees . . . have relevant skills, often obtained through vocational training." As industries transform, she says, work is being created that "demands new skills—which in turn requires new approaches to education, training, and recruiting."[2]

What are those new approaches? IBM intended to hire six thousand employees by the end of 2017, many of whom would have unconventional backgrounds. "About 15 percent of the people we hire in the US don't have four-year degrees," said IBM's former vice president of talent, Joanna Daly. "There's an opportunity to broaden the candidates to fill the skills gap."[3] IBM also announced that it would be partnering with community colleges across the United States to better prepare more Americans for "new collar career opportunities."[4] For those without a formal bachelor's degree, Daly said she looks for hands-on experience and enrollment in relevant vocational classes. Today, more than 50 percent of positions at IBM do not have a degree requirement as the company increases its focus on skills.

A recent study by Deloitte revealed that 90 percent of executives say they are now experimenting with skills-powered approaches across various workforce practices.[5] That same study showed that such organizations are 63 percent more likely to achieve results across eleven key business and workforce metrics, including being more likely to place talent effectively and being more likely to innovate.

At the height of the pandemic, companies as diverse as Verizon and Bank of America saw the benefits of having skills-powered architectures to redeploy talent at speed and scale. Verizon redirected nearly twenty thousand affected store-based employees to leverage their skills in other roles, such as telesales or online customer service. Bank of America redeployed thirty thousand employees to deal with the influx of calls and digital customer inquiries resulting from the passage of the Coronavirus Aid, Relief, and Economic Security Act, which provided emergency payments to individuals and small businesses to counter the economic fallout from the COVID-19 pandemic, in the United States.

Defining and Assessing Skills

For the purposes of this book, we will use the term "skills" as a broad frame and means for capturing an individual's skills (i.e., the theoretical ability to execute a task) *and* their expression of those skills in the form of capabilities that result in the proficient execution of work. The two broad categories of skills are technical (often called hard) skills and human (often called enabling or soft) skills. Technical skills include accounting, coding, welding, and UX design, while human skills include critical thinking, emotional intelligence, problem-solving, and communication. We are often asked about the differences between competencies and skills and find the definition by Degreed helpful in differentiating the two. A competency is defined as knowledge, behaviors, attitudes, and even skills that lead to the ability to do something successfully or efficiently. The ability to make business decisions would be a competency. A skill is defined as learned and applied abilities that use one's knowledge effectively in execution or performance. Using the same example of making business decisions, to do so, you would have to maintain specific skills to perform well: budgeting, market research, and competitive strategy.

Skills are uncovered and measured in various ways, from traditional assessments and tests to feedback from peers and colleagues to, increasingly, inferences by machine learning. Think of skills as falling into two buckets: those verified through certifications and assessments and those unverified due to being inferred by AI or because someone tells you they have those skills. In a perfect world, we would all be unbiased judges of our particular skills. But we know through countless studies that we as a species regularly discount our skills. We often think because we can do something well, everyone else can too. For example, SkyHive, an award-winning Canadian technology company, has found that when people self-report their skills, they typically identify 11 skills, on average, for their particular role. However, when we use SkyHive's technology to infer people's skills from their current and previous roles, experiences, and education, that number jumps to 34.[6] SkyHive and other tech companies are using the power of AI to exponentially advance what we know about skills and how we use them to power the next generation of enterprises. This is something we will explore in more detail in chapter 5.

When we talk about skills, it is important to distinguish between skill acquisition or possession versus expression. We are using the phrase "skills expression" to ensure a connection to work outcomes. We are often asked how experience plays into the expression of skills, and our response is that experience is merely a reflection of the passage of time and not a proxy for the proficiency with which a skill is expressed. Adopting and adapting a framework developed by John Boudreau and Pete Ramstad in their book *Beyond HR*, we think of three ways in which to assess how a skill is expressed:[7]

1. Is the skill expressed efficiently (i.e., the outcome is achieved without wasted effort or "stress" to other individuals or parts of a process)?
2. Is the skill expressed effectively (i.e., the desired outcome is achieved)?
3. Is the skill expressed impactfully (i.e., it achieves the outcome, and the process of expression enhances the experience of others or the achievement of a broader goal)?

What This Book Is About

This book will give business leaders the tools to transform their outdated and traditional work frameworks and systems based on static "jobs" and "employees in jobs." It will show how they can remake those systems and frameworks to make skills the currency of work—with talent and work flowing to each other based on the seamless matching of skills and tasks. The transition to a skills-powered organization will transform every aspect of planning, acquiring, deploying, developing, and managing their workforces.

In *Lead the Work*, Ravin Jesuthasan, John Boudreau, and David Creelman first highlighted the importance of "work deconstruction" and the emerging role of skills as the currency of work.[8] They showed that engaging workers through avenues such as contracting, freelancing, project-based platforms, sharing talent across organizations, tours of duty, crowdsourcing, and volunteers all require optimizing the individual work elements of a traditional "job" and seeing workers in terms of their skills/capabilities rather than simply their qualifications as "employees" assigned to "jobs."

Lead the Work showed how deconstructing work and focusing on skills was essential to uncovering new options for sourcing, rewarding, and engaging workers, with some work elements best done by regular full-time employees. In contrast, others are best done by freelancers, contractors, volunteers, gamers, or others. The framework and cases showed how work deconstruction was fundamental to optimizing worker engagement to revolutionize the cost, risk, and capability profiles of organizations.

Reinventing Jobs, by Jesuthasan and Boudreau, extended these ideas to encompass work automation.[9] It demonstrated that virtually every scientific study of work automation shows that the result will rarely be "employees in jobs replaced by automation." Instead, work automation can only be optimized by understanding how humans and automation will be combined, with humans doing some tasks and automation doing others. Again, work and worker deconstruction to get to the elemental tasks and skills underpinning work were essential to the framework that enables leaders to understand and anticipate how automation might replace, augment, or reinvent human work. Leaders trapped in the typical framework of "jobs" and "employees" will be unprepared to understand work automation, let alone optimize it. *Reinventing Jobs* provided a framework, toolkit, and over one hundred examples and cases illustrating how to deconstruct jobs, analyze the component tasks and skills, distribute those tasks between humans and automation, and then reconstruct them to reveal new and enhanced "reinvented" work.

In their *Wall Street Journal* bestseller, *Work without Jobs*, Jesuthasan and Boudreau further detailed a new work operating system based on deconstructed jobs, skills, and capabilities—which is essential to powering the agile enterprise.[10] Using many examples, they illustrated the new work operating system in action and the implications for leadership, organizational design, and the HR processes required to thrive in an emerging world of perpetual work reinvention.

This book builds on these concepts and ideas to explore the potential for a game-changing evolution to skills-powered organizations—for more inclusive, equitable, and higher-performing enterprises. It also discusses why the conditions are ripe for this transition to a skills-powered organization given the advances in AI, the evolving demands of the workforce, and the changing organizational requirements for greater resilience and agility in a volatile world. Perhaps more importantly, this book will explore both the theory underpinning the skills-powered organization and the practical realities of bringing it to life. Tanuj's unique perspectives as chief strategy and talent officer of Standard Chartered, and having steered the bank on this journey, will provide deep insight into the changes required in terms of mindset, skill set, and toolset.

After reading this book, leaders will understand and be more prepared to successfully build an enterprise with skills as its fundamental component. We will show how they can realize the power of skills as the currency of work using well-grounded and practical approaches that transform how they plan for, acquire, deploy, develop, and manage their investment in their workforces and work. We will illustrate this with a deep dive into Standard Chartered's journey, dissecting various aspects in each chapter, along with numerous case studies from other industries.

So how did we get here? To truly understand the evolution of work and what led us to this point requires us to look back in time and understand how the core building blocks of work have changed. Figure 0.1 depicts the evolution of work over the course of the last three industrial revolutions and the journey to making skills the currency of work.

The Evolution to a Skills-Powered Organization: A Quick Retrospective

The work construct most of us have today is about 140 years old. It is at least as old as the Second Industrial Revolution (1870–1930), when employers aggregated disparate activities into jobs, jobs into job families, and job families into functions. With its relentless pursuit of efficiency, Frederick Taylor's scientific management method (his book, *The Principles of Scientific Management*[11] from 1909, was named the most influential book of the twentieth century by the Academy of Management) was widely embraced. His approach ensured that workers would know exactly what was expected of them and managers would know exactly how much should be produced in an era where capabilities were primarily built and owned by individual companies.

The "one-to-one" relationship between a person and a position was thus born with much of the organization's control systems: finance, HR, and technology, grounded in the notion of the job as the currency of work. Talent was attracted, engaged, and retained with one-size-fits-most approaches that only varied as one ascended the organizational hierarchy (i.e., moving from a "small job" to a "bigger job"). The technology of this era significantly reduced inequality as traditional "craft-based activities," which required high skill premiums and years of expertise and were increasingly automated. This resulted in the democratization of opportunity as skills premiums were reduced, enabling those with "lesser" skills to engage with well-paying work.

In the Third Industrial Revolution (1955–2005), this carefully constructed value chain started to unravel. The democratization of information enabled companies to understand the cost, capabilities, and risks of

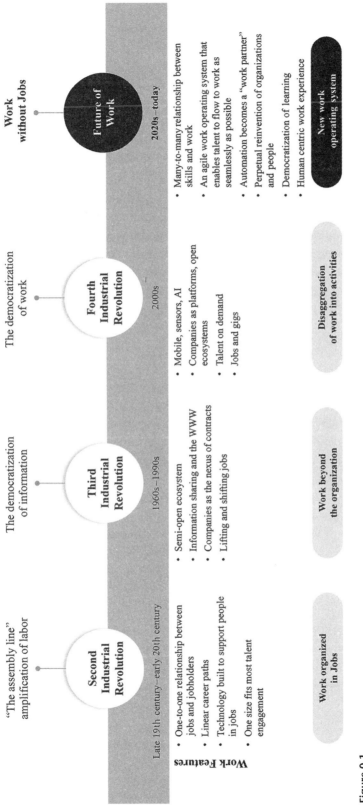

Figure 0.1

The journey to becoming a skills-powered enterprise. *Source:* Ravin Jesuthasan.

working elsewhere. This led to the outsourcing movement as entire jobs and processes were "lifted and shifted" in pursuit of labor arbitrage and greater agility for an increasingly volatile world. In this era, as capabilities were increasingly shared at lower marginal costs, the job continued to serve as the primary currency of work. The end of this era saw significant advances in computers but also resulted in greater inequality. Research by David Autor and others observed significant "job polarization" during this time.[12] Computers increased wages and opportunities for high-income, college-educated workers—substituting a range of highly rules-based work in manufacturing and offices that had once provided solid opportunities for people without a college degree.

In the Fourth Industrial Revolution (2005–present), advances in cloud-based computing, mobile technology, and AI heralded the democratization of work—our growing ability to increasingly decouple work from its traditional confines of space, time, and structure. As companies increasingly turned to platform-based business models that allowed them to engage with talent on demand, the concept of gig work was born. This started the move toward skills serving as the currency of work instead of jobs.

In this era, capabilities are increasingly rented when needed, at virtually zero fixed cost. The inequality in wages and opportunities that started in the 1990s has been exacerbated in this era. Repetitive, rules-based work has diminished, and with the augmentation of technology, an even greater premium has been placed on reasoning, decision-making, abstract thinking, problem-solving, and creativity.

As we approach a post–Fourth Industrial Revolution world, we see that the demands of the agile movement, the recent advances in generative AI, the need for greater flexibility in business models, and increased economic volatility further accelerate the need for skills as the currency of work to ensure the rapid (re)deployment of talent to changing demands for work. The World Economic Forum's *Future of Jobs Report 2023* suggested that 60 percent of workers will require additional training by 2027—with the biggest priority being analytical thinking.[13] Technology-related roles dominated the report's list of fastest-growing jobs, with AI and machine learning specialists at the top. While there is undoubtedly a rapidly growing premium for all talent to become "AI-fluent," the obsession with developing programming skills might not last given the dramatic advances we are seeing with generative AI and large language models. These advancements are increasingly making English the dominant programming language, further democratizing knowledge and creativity by enabling more and more people to harness the power of AI. Interestingly, this democratization may have the benefit of reducing the rising inequality we have experienced over the last two Industrial Revolutions. This is because generative AI increases the productivity of talent with lesser skills, much as the automation of the Second Industrial Revolution did.

Even as it accelerates the need for skills, AI is proving to be a powerful resource in generating the insights and capabilities needed to enable upskilling, reskilling, and talent redeployment at scale and speed. AI algorithms can analyze the skills required for talent to perform various tasks, infer the workforce's skills, and identify skills adjacencies and interventions to close skill gaps. For example, data scientists are reskilling to perform machine learning work. By moving beyond jobs to skills, companies can redeploy talent more seamlessly.

The World Economic Forum's "Putting Skills First: A Framework for Action" suggests that a "skills-first" approach to hiring and developing people can transform labor markets, delivering significant benefits to business and society.[14] It means businesses get the skills they actually need for a particular body of work (instead of relying on imprecise markers of capabilities like degrees.) Further, it democratizes access to work for those with those skills regardless of how they acquired them. The report suggests that across the eighteen economies analyzed, more than one hundred million people could be added to the global talent pool through a skills-first approach. The advances in Web3 are further accelerating new models for connecting talent to work in distributed autonomous organizations (DAOs), which will further democratize access to work and prioritize using skills as the currency of work.

Let's explore Standard Chartered's journey against this general context, using its story to illustrate how we have advanced to this precipice of the skills-powered organization.

Standard Chartered's Journey to Becoming a Skills-Powered Organization

Standard Chartered is a 170-year-old, leading international banking group, with more than eighty-five thousand employees across over fifty of the world's most dynamic markets and serving clients in a further sixty-four.

For Standard Chartered, the skills-powered journey started with transitioning the narrative from jobs to skills. It began with a very commercial business case based on its own strategic workforce planning analysis, highlighting the jobs within the organization that would soon no longer be relevant (which it refers to as "sunset" roles). This might be due to changing client expectations or the evolution of technology and automation of tasks. New jobs would also be created as a result ("sunrise" roles). The strategic workforce plan (SWP) also highlighted the broader impact of the changing demand for skills—the disproportionate displacement of junior roles and the resulting cost implications as the organization shifted from a pyramid to a diamond shape. Additionally, it highlighted the potential impact on gender diversity due to the higher number of women currently employed in sunset roles and with many sunrise roles being currently more male dominated. The tangible economics of "build" versus "buy," and the far-reaching impact of decisions related to upskilling and reskilling, created a compelling foundation for the board and the global management team (i.e., the senior most executive team composed of the global CEO, CFO, business/function/region heads), and it continues to drive their sponsorship of the skills journey.

A first step at Standard Chartered has been the goal of "building a learning habit" and directing this focus toward priority skills and work of the future, as well as recognizing that this future lies in a combination of technical skills and human skills. Core to building the learning habit—across an eighty-five-thousand-strong workforce in over fifty markets worldwide—has been the ability to leverage technology to democratize access to skill development. That has meant access to rich, on-demand content and cross-functional, cross-geography developmental experiences that enable building, practicing, and honing skills through projects. As employees started to build this muscle (as evidenced by an increase in bank-wide average learning days from 2.8 in 2019 to 4.7 in 2022), a range of targeted proof-of-concept (POC) experiments were also launched to build talent pipelines for priority sunrise roles. This was done using a data-led approach to identify potential colleagues for reskilling and upskilling opportunities based on skills adjacency while targeting talent in the aforementioned sunset roles.

As further progress was made in building the skills of the future across its workforce, the organization became equally conscious of a need to deploy these skills in an accelerated manner to the areas of greatest demand and opportunity. The AI-based internal talent marketplace it has implemented enables the identification of the top skills in demand and the talent possessing those skills, seamlessly matching and deploying skills across functional and geographic boundaries. As they continues to scale the use of this technology, the long-term vision is for the marketplace to become the "golden source" of skills information, development, and deployment. This will help it capture, track, and manage the supply and demand for skills on a real-time basis.

Labor shortages and other factors have increasingly shifted the balance of power from employers to employees over the past few years, and the journey to becoming a skills-powered organization has proven to be both a significant asset in future-proofing the Standard Chartered's business model and a massive contributor to its employee value proposition (EVP). The "war for talent" is a war for future skills that will disproportionately impact business growth and client outcomes. Moreover, the workforce increasingly wants to have a voice in what work they do, where it is done, when it is done, how it is done, who it is done by (including automation), and why it is done. They want a variety of opportunities and want to work for organizations that allow them to grow their skills. This demands increasing agility—at the organizational and individual level—to allow the seamless flow of talent and skills to work and opportunity.

As the development and deployment of skills has become increasingly democratized across the firm, it is also mindful that its people and operational practices and processes also need to keep pace. These include embedding a skills mindset into talent decisions by increasing internal certifications and visibility of external accreditations to ensure a robust and reliable view of the skills attained by an individual, and eventually using the concept of a "skills passport" to drive greater internal mobility. These steps and others are all part of the journey toward making skills the currency of work across Standard Chartered.

The Journey to Becoming a Skills-Powered Organization, Its Foundational Elements, and Their Evolution

In the following chapters, we delve further into the journey at Standard Chartered and other organizations, discussing the critical elements of the skills-powered organization and how it will evolve. Chapter 1 explores the foundational elements underpinning the skills-powered organization and the differentiated capabilities required to lead it. It also examines the key leadership mechanisms and the five new skills required of leaders. In chapter 2 we discuss how the organization is being reinvented with skills as the currency of work, exploring three alternative models for organizing work and their significant consequences for organizational performance and the human experience of work. We also explore why a skills-powered construct is essential to enabling an agile, team-driven organization.

Chapter 3 illustrates the changing work experience for talent that results from the evolution to the skills-powered organization. It also explores why a skills-powered foundation is essential to delivering an ethical, equitable, and inclusive work experience. Chapter 4 explores the three critical organizational capabilities underpinning the skills-powered organization. This chapter also illustrates the transformative changes required of legacy infrastructure and routines that have shaped 140 years of work being organized as jobs. Chapter 5 discusses how AI is accelerating and enabling this journey, exploring the evolution of multiple skills insights and marketplace platforms and their increasingly pivotal role in powering this journey, including the accelerative implications of generative AI.

We then shift our attention in chapter 6 to exploring the crucial role of the function formerly known as HR in powering and governing this journey as human work and AI become inextricably woven together. In chapter 7, we examine how the shift to skills as the currency of work is enabling a more seamless talent ecosystem comprising various types of employee and nonemployee labor. We also explore the evolving role of different stakeholders and the efforts by governments around the world to prepare their citizens for this next era of work. We conclude in chapter 8 with a call to action for leaders and talent at all levels, providing a detailed roadmap and examples to shape their path to building and leading the skills-powered organization and enabling them to thrive individually in a skills-powered world.

1 Defining and Leading the Skills-Powered Organization

In today's rapidly changing and competitive job market, skills have become the new currency of work. The days when a college degree was singularly sufficient in securing a job are increasingly a thing of the past. Now, employers are looking for candidates with diverse skills that can adapt to the ever-evolving business landscape. Why is that?

1. The rise of technology and automation has significantly impacted the job market, leading to a shift in the skills employers seek. According to the World Economic Forum, some of the top skills that will be in demand in the next decade include complex problem-solving, critical thinking, creativity, people management, emotional intelligence, and cognitive flexibility.[1] These skills are not only in demand in industries such as technology and finance but are also becoming increasingly important in fields such as healthcare and education. LinkedIn's skills-first report previously found that its members have seen the skills of their jobs change by 25 percent since 2015.[2] At that rate, workers could expect their jobs to change by nearly 60 percent by 2030. However, with new generative AI technologies and tools emerging every day, LinkedIn now forecasts the pace and scale of change to jobs to accelerate even more—by an additional 5 percentage points—to reach at least 65 percent by 2030.

2. With the rise of the gig economy and remote work, employees are expected to be more versatile and adaptable than ever before. Freelancers and independent contractors must be able to wear multiple hats and have a wide range of skills to stay competitive. Employers are increasingly looking for candidates with strong digital skills, including social media skills, the ability to navigate online tools and platforms, and, more recently, the skills to work with generative AI and large language models as these technologies increasingly permeate the workplace.

3. The emphasis on skills has also led to a shift in how education is approached. Traditional four-year degrees are no longer seen as the only path to a successful career. Short-term courses and boot camps that focus on developing specific technical skills such as coding, data analysis, and digital marketing have become increasingly popular, providing an alternative route to gaining the necessary skills for employment.

4. In addition to being a key factor in securing employment, having diverse skills also allows individuals to be more adaptable and resilient in their careers. As industries evolve and new technologies emerge, those with a broad skill set are better equipped to pivot and stay relevant in their fields.

5. However, acquiring and maintaining diverse skills can be a daunting task. It requires a commitment to lifelong learning and continuous skill development. Fortunately, the rise of online learning platforms and the availability of free or low-cost courses have made it easier than ever to acquire new skills. This does require the thoughtful orchestration and sequencing of the optimal portfolio of bite-sized learning resources.

6. Equally important, the attitudes of talent toward work are changing dramatically. In McKinsey's 2022 "American Opportunity Survey," Gen Z respondents who were working were more likely to have independent jobs or multiple jobs than older workers, with 28 percent choosing independent work or gigs because they enjoyed the work and 24 percent due to the autonomy and flexibility it afforded.[3]

As employers place increasing value on individuals with a diverse skill set who can adapt to changing industry demands, we are seeing the shift toward skills-powered employment, leading to a new focus on lifelong learning and continuous skill development and providing individuals with the tools they need to stay competitive in the labor market.

But Why Now for Skills and Are All Skills the Same?

Several factors are driving the need for skills as the currency of work. According to the World Economic Forum, recent developments have contributed to the emergence of skills-powered talent management practices.[4] These include labor shortages in various economies and sectors, increased remote work and changes in talent management practices during the COVID-19 pandemic, the growth of online learning and microcredentials, and increasingly sophisticated tools for jobs and skills mapping. Having the right skills within an organization also remains a critical concern for companies as they look to reinvent their business model, reduce costs, and manage external economic pressures in an ever more volatile, digitally enabled world.

Recent research by Dave Ulrich and Norm Smallwood, in collaboration with Amazon Web Services, builds a strong case for skills.[5] It has shown that human capability—defined as the combination of talent (skills), leadership, organization, and HR—accounts for 44.5 percent of revenue per employee and 26 percent of earnings (EBITDA) across 5,760 organizations reporting to the Securities and Exchange Commission.

In the *How Skills Are Disrupting Work* report from the Burning Glass Institute, Business-Higher Education Forum, and Wiley, the authors paint an intriguing picture of the changing trajectory and velocity of skills:

The demand for new skills is spreading rapidly across all sectors. Not long ago, the need for new skills was concentrated in the tech sector. However, the spread of the demand for new skills is transforming industries and sectors, rendering some skills virtually ubiquitous. In 2011, for instance, there were 294,000 job posts seeking people with data analysis skills in only 17 occupations; 10 years later, 1.2 million such jobs were posted in 81 occupations. Many of the skills are spreading to existing jobs, where workers have to learn and apply them, but the spread is also happening in new occupations created by these evolving skills.

Work increasingly demands skills from across domains. Many skills invading jobs also cross-functional silos, requiring workers to exercise unfamiliar skills. Right-brain marketing people now need the left-brain analytical skills to make sense of and manipulate customer data. For example, 1 in 12 marketing jobs demanded data skills in 2013; now that number is 1 in 8. In design, the number has shifted from 1 in 20 to 1 in 13. By contrast, digitally skilled engineers and data analysts increasingly need management, communications, or design skills to function in a collaborative workplace. The number of occupations with 2,000 or more job postings requesting creativity rose from 12 in 2012 to 55 in 2022, including roles like Computer Systems Engineers, IT Project Managers, and Program Managers.

Emerging skills bring both an opportunity for innovation and a threat of obsolescence. For those who can acquire new skills rapidly and continuously, there are powerful opportunities to make discoveries, lead industries, and excel. But skills disruptions also raise the risk of a new, more subtle form of obsolescence for all parties. Workers who have performed in a role for years may find that what is expected has changed so much that they lack the skills required to do that job going forward, particularly if they lose a long-held job and try finding a new one. At the same time, as employers redefine roles and seek to stay ahead of disruptions, they may find that the workforce they have is no longer the workforce they will need going forward. Educators face a daunting challenge: They must keep their finger on the pulse of new skills demands, and look ahead as best they can, to develop learning opportunities for workers and students that will meet the future needs of employers.

Digital skills are among the fastest-growing and most rapidly spreading skills. A very large proportion of emerging skills are digital—there is a high correlation between the clusters of skills in greatest demand and those that rely heavily on technology. In the Skills Disruption Matrix developed by the Burning Glass Institute with BCG [Boston Consulting Group] and Lightcast, more than 75% of the most disrupted occupations were digital or technological.[6]

As you can see, the dramatic changes in demand for various skills are a function of the shrinking half-life of many technical skills—due to rapid advances in automation and the democratization of work. But just how fast is this happening? The *2023 Skills Compass Report* by the Burning Glass Institute and Coursera sheds some light on this. According to Matt Sigelman, president of the Burning Glass Institute, 37 percent of the average job's skills have been replaced over the past five years.[7] Such a pace of change makes it difficult for individuals and companies to determine which skills to invest in or how different training options will pay off.

The *Skills Compass Report* uses data on the longevity and market value of essential skills to present learning implementation recommendations. Skills such as cloud computing, engineering, AI, machine learning, communications, and problem-solving are quantified across three dimensions to better understand how and how much to invest in them:

- **Time to skill:** Measures the time required to become proficient in a particular skill
- **Skill value:** Calculates the average salary in the market for that skill
- **Skill longevity:** Assesses how long a skill is considered relevant to the market after that skill has been acquired

Through this analysis, Coursera and Burning Glass Institute have articulated the investment thesis behind common skill "types" so leaders and HR can determine how to prioritize, invest, and deploy critical capabilities in their organization. The skills measured landed in five distinct themes:

- **Solid investment:** The cost and time it takes to acquire these skills is typically high, but their longevity is also high. This includes skills like risk management and project management as they are particularly durable and costly to develop while not being quite as expensive to hire.

- **Quick dividend:** These skills have medium-to-high longevity but are also unique since they are often less expensive to learn than they are to hire for. For example, Salesforce administration and data structure skills are technical skills that can pay dividends over many years and are less difficult to learn.

- **Enduring:** Skills in this category have very high longevity and are often extremely low cost to hire for or develop. Investing in skills like teamwork or research delivers a high return on investment (ROI) as they are fairly quick to acquire while still having high longevity.

- **Adaptive:** These skills are costly to hire and expensive to acquire. Unlike solid investment skills, adaptive skills don't have the same level of longevity. This category includes technical skills like Swift and network security, which require constant updating and education to keep pace with changes.

- **Commodity:** These are widely acquired skills that are often inexpensive to acquire through hiring. Historically, these are skills that have been around for many years. Some examples are web development and cascading style sheets.

Creating an enterprise that can adapt to these rapidly changing and nuanced scenarios and use them for competitive advantage will be essential to ensuring its ongoing resilience and agility.

So, What Does the Skills-Powered Organization Look Like?

Skills-powered organizations differ from traditional companies in several ways, including their organizational structure, approach to recruitment and hiring, and emphasis on skill development.

1. Organizational structure: Skills-powered organizations tend to have flatter organizational structures, with less hierarchy and more cross-functional teams. They focus on collaboration, communication, and knowledge sharing across teams to promote continuous learning and

development. This structure enables employees to develop a broader skill set and encourages a culture of innovation and experimentation.

2. Talent acquisition: Skills-powered organizations prioritize skills and potential over traditional metrics such as education and experience. They may use skills assessments, competency-based interviews, and work samples to evaluate candidates' skills and potential. This approach allows them to identify candidates with the skills needed to succeed in a particular role regardless of their educational background or work experience.

3. Emphasis on skill development: Skills-powered organizations prioritize skill development, providing employees with opportunities to learn and develop new skills. They invest in employee training and development programs, mentoring, and job shadowing to promote continuous learning and growth. This approach helps employees stay current with the latest industry trends and develop a broad skill set, making them more adaptable and resilient in their careers.

4. Emphasis on diversity and inclusion: Skills-powered organizations prioritize diversity and inclusion, recognizing that a diverse workforce brings different perspectives and experiences that can drive innovation and growth. They create a culture that values diversity and promotes equity and inclusion, helping attract and retain a diverse workforce.

5. Agile and adaptable: Skills-powered organizations are agile and adaptable, able to pivot quickly to changing industry demands. They prioritize innovation and experimentation, encouraging employees to take risks and try new things. This approach allows organizations to stay ahead of the competition and adapt to changing market conditions.

So, if this defines a skills-powered organization, how do you become one? What is required to power the transformation of your organization toward being a skills-powered organization? In our estimation, seven critical factors underpin the skills-powered organization:

1. Leadership mechanisms and skills: The leaders of skills-powered organizations operate in fundamentally different ways. They lead in five unique ways and demonstrate five distinct skills, which we will explore in this chapter.

2. Agility in the organizational model: A more nuanced organizational structure is required to enable the transition to skills as the currency of

work and optimize how talent is connected to work. We will explore the emerging organizational constructs in chapter 2.

3. Reinvention of the work experience: The transition from jobs to skills as the currency of work creates the opportunity to reenvision the legacy one-size-fits-all employment experience and its underlying talent model. We will discuss this in chapter 3.

4. Development of new organizational capabilities: The skills-powered organization is underpinned by several distinct capabilities like reinvented talent processes to acquire, develop, deploy, and reward skills and work design as a pivotal capability. We will illustrate these in detail in chapter 4.

5. Leveraging the power of AI: AI is a pivotal tool for shifting from the one-to-one relationship between jobs and jobholders to the many-to-many between skills and work. The ability to deploy AI at scale and thoughtfully (and responsibly) manage data is critical. We discuss this in detail in chapter 5.

6. Reinvention of the HR function: As with any transformative change, the HR function plays a pivotal in the journey to the skills-powered organization. However, its structure, capabilities, and operating model need to be radically different. We explore this in chapter 6.

7. Thinking beyond the organization: The skills-powered organization is increasingly characterized by its ability to tap into a broader talent ecosystem beyond employees or traditional contractors. We will illustrate this in chapter 7.

Let's now explore what leadership of a skills-powered organization looks like.

Leadership Mechanisms and Skills

Leading a skills-powered organization requires some different mechanisms and skills. Let's start with the mechanisms. As described by Ravin Jesuthasan and John Boudreau in *Reinventing Jobs*, the five mechanisms that redefine leadership are the following:[8]

1. Mindset: From "learn, do, retire" to "learn, do, learn, do, rest, learn . . . repeat"

2. Ability: From employment qualifications to work readiness

3. Reward: From salaries for permanent jobs to flexible total rewards for deconstructed work and skills

4. Deployment: From job architecture and movement between jobs to work architecture that continuously matches skills to work

5. Development: From career ladders based on fixed jobs to reskilling pathways based on tasks and reinvented jobs

Let's explore each of these in detail:

Mindset

In his 1970 bestseller *Future Shock*, Alvin Toffler wrote that "the illiterate of the 21st century will not be those who cannot read and write, but those who cannot learn, unlearn, and relearn." His observation becomes more relevant every day. The great twentieth-century giants like General Motors and Ford grew by aggregating individual craftsmen in cottage industries into jobs in centralized factories. For decades, the careers that created income during employment and retirement comprised those jobs. Predictability and stability allowed schools to train talent before employment, organizations to add additional long-term skills, and careers to progress consistently through job families organized into functions like research and design, manufacturing, HR, finance, and sales. Authority and accountability predictably progressed from individual contributor to supervisor to executive. This linear progression worked during times of predictable and relatively stable economic growth and supported organizations at a global scale with hundreds of thousands of employees. Perhaps the most vivid icons of this stability were the defined benefit retirement pension and medical plans, made possible by predictable growth and shorter life spans.

Of course, modern reality could not be more different. The volatile, uncertain, complex, and ambiguous modern world is amplified by rampant digitalization and automation, geopolitical conflict, the democratization of work, and the aftereffects of the COVID-19 pandemic. This reality is often recognized in decisions about money, technology, innovation, customers, and markets. We see it in the shrinking half-life of skills and the relentless reinvention of jobs. These changes in work combine with societal trends such as increased life expectancy, ubiquitous virtual connectivity, social media, cyber threats, and income inequality. Past generations could rely on rewards from a pattern of "learn, do, retire," but that no longer holds. Jobs and professions have a shorter half-life even as the duration of our work lives increases. The new pattern will reflect a series of different work experiences built upon projects and shorter tours of duty in each organization. That requires a mindset more like "learn, do, learn, do, rest, learn . . . repeat."

Ability

Employment qualifications are often defined using technical skills, a concern shared by employers and policymakers as companies find it challenging to locate workers with the full set of skills required for today's work. To address this, governments and educational institutions try to identify and provide all those skills to reduce the gaps between being technically qualified to being work ready. However, as value shifts from technical to human skills, education, training, and learning must retool accordingly. Workers can increasingly acquire technical skills quickly and cheaply outside of employment or educational institutions. For example, LinkedIn Learning has all the courses needed to qualify as a Python developer. It offers learning pathways for many technical skills (Java, graphic design, 3D animation, network/infrastructure administration, etc.), and it is only one such source.

Online learning sources also give workers a clear understanding of skill adjacencies. For example, graphic design and 3D animation are adjacent skills because the work of graphic design can be upskilled to 3D animation work. On the other hand, although they share some common attributes, Python programming is not closely related to graphic design. It takes many more hours and a longer pathway to go from Python to 3D animation even though 3D animation may be done on software that uses Python programming. Leaders must understand such relationships and offer workers the most effective learning path even if that means leaving their organization. Learning is integrated with rewards by combining an online talent platform like Upwork with the online learning solutions of LinkedIn Learning. Now, a Java programmer on Upwork can earn $30 per hour but can easily see that Android programmers earn $35 per hour. LinkedIn Learning shows them they can become certified Android programmers with four additional courses over fourteen hours.

When the price and alignment of such skill pathways are so apparent, leaders can and must shift their focus from searching for fully prepared candidates to searching for those who are optimally close to being qualified and strategies to optimize the work and worker to achieve the most efficient match. Automation plays into this in two ways: it accelerates the continual evolution toward new skills and provides the means to acquire and demonstrate those skills. As technical skills become increasingly easy to obtain and change, leaders will expect educational institutions—and their organization's long-term training and development—to reinvent themselves, focusing on enabling skills. This is made more consistent and accessible by creating robust skills taxonomies like those of the World Economic Forum, which are available to all companies. Leaders must enable relationships with workers that span multiple engagements, punctuated by workers leaving to acquire new skills through education or work with other organizations. They must also learn to identify and track enabling capabilities, even among workers who may not currently possess the formal certifications or degrees in required technical areas. The best talent may be a worker with an amazing ability to learn and see connections but whose technical qualifications don't yet match the organization's current needs.

Reward

Typically, organizations value and reward work by combining tasks into a job and then surveying a market of rewards for comparable jobs in comparable organizations. Data from online sites such as salary.com and LinkedIn has increasingly modernized the process. Certainly, a worker's rewards reflect personal attributes like experience and "hot skills" like Python programming, but the rewards are typically attached to a job. This is even true when workers are engaged through arrangements other than regular full-time employment because the requisitions for contractors or freelancers are often based on jobs.

So, how can work be valued in this new world of skills? Organizations like Mercer have developed skills-powered compensation pricing tools that enable discrete skills to be valued. In addition, a market for deconstructed tasks can be much more efficient, as talent platforms already show. If you want to engage an Android app developer, you can go to Upwork, Toptal, or other such platforms and immediately find an array of developers and current pay rates, with the range reflecting their different past performance ratings, experience, and current expertise. The prices for the tasks of Android app development, and even the language to describe the work, all change quickly as the skills required change, as parts of the work are automated, and as workers respond by changing their skills. Because the unit of analysis is the deconstructed work task and not the job, these markets support a higher volume and velocity of transactions as workers and employers discover work tasks that they can substitute or augment with automation. Moreover, as automation creates entirely new versions of the work, a market freed from job descriptions and indexed to skills can adapt more easily and quickly. This adaptation reflects more than merely how much a task is valued. The market can also differentiate rewards to reflect the location, independence, continuity, reputation, and even how the work supports missions such as environmental sustainability, social justice, and so on.

How does this reward system change leadership? Leaders and workers will more constantly negotiate and renegotiate the nature and rewards of work, because work and jobs will be perpetually reinvented and the skills required will change. Those reward negotiations will focus on deconstructed and reconstructed tasks to optimize automation and different ways of connecting talent to work. Both leaders and workers will increasingly have access to the same information, a far different situation than that in which only the leader knows organizational pay levels and only the workers know their true skills and alternatives.

Deployment

Traditionally, we deploy talent to jobs using job architectures. A job like "software development engineer" exists in a job family like software development that has multiple engineering jobs and levels. Each higher level has greater scope, impact, and responsibility. Several job families, such as software development and network design, may be grouped into job families, like engineering. Organizations hire and develop workers through jobs and job families, which can be costly and inefficient. Moreover, as we have seen, perpetually upgraded or agile work is reinvented too quickly for such fixed and job-based architectures to keep up. Deploying workers from one job to another is also too blunt edged to capture the nuances of deconstruction, reinvention, and work automation.

When the unit of analysis is the work task, more agile knowledge architecture can use data from multiple sources like LinkedIn and Upwork to match worker capabilities to work. As a leader, your relationship with the work and workers changes fundamentally. You oversee deployment options that cross the functional and organizational boundaries, and your role is not so much to match workers with their next job but rather to optimize worker development to fit perpetual work evolution. You will increasingly look for workers who closely match the required skills, even if they are not perfect fits, and deploy them to projects so they can develop targeted skills. Additionally, you'll use the language of jobs less often and use the language of deconstructed tasks, automation, and workers' skills more often. As job architectures enabled the organizations of the Second Industrial Revolution, the deconstructed task and skill architecture form the basis for the more connected work ecosystems that will likely characterize a post–Fourth Industrial Revolution world.

Development

How do we then ensure the continued reskilling of humans? In the past, stable economic environments and technology allowed development within specific professional domains and a single organization. Accountants built a base of technical skills and then took additional classes and a progression of jobs to expand them. They might have started a career doing financial reporting in a corporation and then shifted to working as an auditor with a large accounting firm, leveraging knowledge of US accounting laws and regulations. Then, they might have shifted into consulting on management accounting, building on their knowledge to add skills in accounting principles outside the United States. This journey followed a predictable and stable path to build and enhance technical skills that were easily verified and tracked.

In the future, such technical skills will change more quickly, often replaced or altered as the work combines with automation. Moreover, those changes will be difficult to predict far in advance. Human skills will last longer, but workers must develop technical and human skills and adjust to career paths and learning pathways that change quickly. As a leader, you will play a key role in whether the future of work and automation means the demise of learning and development within organizations or the birth of a more precise, comprehensive, and boundless approach. This new approach will better account for the whole worker rather than only those skills and attributes that matter for a particular job or are included in your proprietary organizational skill taxonomy. It's possible to imagine future leaders unconcerned with worker development, relying on the workers themselves to navigate a more transparent system of platforms and online career communities like LinkedIn. However, leaders have the opportunity to create unique worker engagement by guiding them through a connected and evolving array of skill development options, informed by more open work architecture. Leaders in future best places to work will likely become just this sort of skilled guide. Work—automation optimization through deconstruction and job reinvention—will provide leaders with greater insight into where and how automation will replace human labor for specific tasks.

Additionally, reskilling will increasingly rely on human, not technical, skills. The new reskilling pathways will map human skills through many types of work that will span different professional domains, work arrangements, and organizations. In addition to their technical accounting skills, accountants might also possess human skills: a global mindset, a strong process and method orientation, caution and risk aversion, and a learning orientation. Reskilling pathways would track how these skills support the full development path and the new technical skills acquired along the way. An accountant's career might now include managing an oil rig in Saudi Arabia, leading the actuarial function at a global insurer, or operating as an independent quality assessor for a major pharmaceutical company.

These jobs seem very far from the typical career path, yet they each require specific human skills for success. An oil rig manager needs a global mindset to manage a team of workers from around the world, coupled with a process and method orientation to ensure the integrity of highly repetitive, process-based work. In this role, the human skill of caution is critical, as a small mistake can have devastating consequences. Similarly, an actuarial leader benefits from a global mindset in leading a global function, with a process and method orientation playing a key role in maintaining the integrity of tasks such as determining reserves and evaluating claims. Here, caution and risk aversion enhance performance on risk diligence. Meanwhile, an independent quality assessor might apply a global mindset not for supervising an international team but rather for evaluating processes and products in many different countries. For them, process orientation is critical for creating consistent, repeatable processes that can be audited and verified, while the enabling skills of caution and risk aversion are important for establishing appropriate risk tolerances for deviations from established standards. So, what might be the skills that underpin these new ways of working?

Five New Leadership Skills

Many leaders have spent their careers under a work model focused on jobs centered on a command-and-control hierarchy. Reorienting to a more agile, skills-powered model will be a major paradigm shift for them. Furthermore, the future of work requires not only a change of mindset for leaders but also a shift in skill set. What it took to be a successful executive or manager using the old way of work will simply not translate. New skills, social values, and behaviors will be required. In a system of continually reinvented work, there are fewer places for leaders to hide and thus more visibility. The success of leadership will be less defined by title than by projects and accomplishments and, ultimately, character. As we have shown, leaders will need to rethink fundamentals like attracting, retaining, motivating, and engaging workers and will need to attend to their individual leadership brand.

Leaders will want to take this opportunity to reorient around more humanistic leadership. This is because talent will be looking closely at both the task's desirability and the leader's "brand" and reputation. Leaders will continually earn their reputations through their track records and behavior. The most successful leaders—who can best attract talent—will be those who can steadily and sustainably guide the ship and match skills to work. What must leaders adapt to lead a skills-powered organization? As John Boudreau and Ravin Jesuthasan noted in *Work without Jobs*, five fundamental skill shifts must be undertaken.[9]

1. Moving from hierarchical authority to empowerment and alignment: One of the most observable changes in a skills-powered organization is a shift in how work is done. Leaders will need to transition from thinking about how they organize jobs to thinking about how tasks and projects are accomplished. As employees gain the flexibility to shift from project to project based on skills and preferences, leaders must set strong frameworks to balance that empowerment with accountability and create an organization-wide consistency that keeps people aligned with the broader mission. Organization-level leaders will need to focus on how they

   • set the overall strategic mission for the organization;
   • define and prioritize tasks and projects;

- define the standards, goals, conditions, supporting systems, resources, and skills needed to accomplish those tasks; and
- support leaders and managers throughout the organization.

Once these top-level goals and processes are set, functional leaders will establish guardrails and systems to align and support midlevel leaders, focusing on how work is accomplished and shared. Midlevel leaders will then use those guardrails to prioritize and translate organizational goals into strategic objectives and skills required for their units. Front-line managers will continue to define and prioritize the processes, tasks, and skills required to meet team and organizational objectives. At the project level, leaders will deconstruct projects into tasks and tap workers to join their projects and teams based on the skills needed. Workers will no longer be assigned exclusively to one leader or role but will be free-floating. This means that leaders and managers throughout the organization will need to transition from being leaders of people in roles to being leaders of people on projects, organizing and optimizing people and technology around skills and orchestrating resources to accomplish tasks and meet goals.

2. Moving from technical to humanistic work automation: As AI, machine learning, and technologies like ChatGPT-4 and Dall-E 2 continue to transform our work, leaders must balance how humans and automation work together across projects and tasks. This is an advantage skills-powered work has over job-centered work, as optimal solutions for work automation are often visible only at the task and skill level. Looking through this lens will help leaders make better choices regarding how they replace, augment, or reinvent human workers. To successfully make this transition, leaders must come to a more nuanced understanding of what humans bring to the table regarding aesthetic creativity, cultural context, and innovative potential. They must also eliminate biases that assume machines will always produce greater efficiency or consistency.

3. Moving from episodic to continuous focus on diversity, equity, and inclusion (DEI): A large part of the transformation to a skills-powered organization means reorienting around more human social values. Traditional models encourage an episodic view of DEI, but the future of work will be determined by the quality of DEI in ongoing relationships and interactions. In skills-powered organizations, leaders are actively

involved in choosing, assigning, and developing team members, and the focus will be squarely on the substance of those interactions. Each interaction will present an opportunity to enhance DEI or perpetuate existing bias if it persists.

4. Moving from digital savvy to tech fluency: Recent and rapid innovations in areas such as AI and robotics have challenged companies to keep up with rapid process and workflow changes, but combining humans and automation in the ecosystem of work means balancing innovations with viability, practicality, and decisions on the project or task level. This is a symbiotic relationship. Where teams are simultaneously forming and disbanding, algorithms will be at the heart of supervision and coordination, giving leaders the tools and insights they need to stay informed and to determine where or whether automation will replace, augment, or reinvent human work and the skill implications of those choices.

5. Moving from process execution to project guidance: This involves sourcing talent beyond the traditional organization and rapidly assembling teams based on skills using tools that agile teams now use (scrum, sprints, hacks, etc.). Guardrails (HR, IT, legal, compliance, operations finance, etc.) are now set when someone takes a job—clearances, processes, and so on. But as jobs give way to skills as the currency of work, the guardrails will have to be adapted quickly and continually, with cross-functional coordination.

At first, a skills-powered organization may seem to diminish the human dimension of work, but the steps above illustrate how central humanity will be to such an enterprise. To avoid chaos and ensure alignment with a broader strategy, leaders must shift how power and accountability are distributed and evolve to a more agile, serial leadership model that emphasizes their human skills.

Let's explore how Standard Chartered has built its leadership skills.

Building Exponential Leaders at Standard Chartered

Standard Chartered has been on an ambitious growth journey, and its leadership team knew early on that to drive the necessary transformation, all their fourteen thousand managers spanning over fifty markets would be central to the firm's success. The business case for investing in their managers was always very clear. External research empirically links employee satisfaction (of which satisfaction with one's manager is a key driver) with customer satisfaction, profitability, and productivity.[10] The data from their own consumer banking business showed that better leadership was strongly correlated with better feedback from clients.

Deliberate steps were needed to not just build managers' capabilities but also shift mindsets. However, rather than completely redesign a manager's job, Standard Chartered began with a basic step and changed the narrative around the role. The idea that one is called a "manager" while in the middle management level and then becomes a "leader" only as they grow in the organizational hierarchy felt counterintuitive to the change it was driving in its culture. All erstwhile managers are now called "people leaders," giving the cohort an identity not driven by hierarchy. This change was a significant marker of the expectation of them—to lead people and not just manage tasks. The organization then kicked off a three-pronged approach to unlock the potential of its people leaders and others whose roles require them to lead: define, develop, and measure.

This work was done in partnership with a leadership council, chaired by a senior executive and comprising a dozen diverse people leaders from across the firm. The intention was to build, test, and improve the leadership system with and for the leaders, future leaders, and those being led, not simply by imposing static frameworks but by involving leaders and stakeholders in cocreating it. The council was tasked with defining Standard Chartered's leadership aspiration and expectations, overseeing a renewal of how the development of people leaders is supported, and creating a compelling leadership brand identity that enhanced the value proposition.

Defining Leadership at Standard Chartered

A leadership competency framework has been long defined and used by the company to provide consistent language and observable behaviors around leadership. As it continued to transform, the organization decided to take the positive leadership lessons emerging from the COVID-19 pandemic and its strategic ambition for the future to create a differentiated, more human leadership identity. It wanted to create leaders who aspire for more, inspire others, and execute the strategy for its clients, teams, and communities. So, with input from the broader employee base, the leadership council cocreated the "leadership agreement," which calls out the leadership ambition and sets clear expectations of the leadership standards needed to drive and accelerate performance.[11] These are defined by fourteen practices that underpin the agreement that all leaders are expected to role model as they "aspire," "inspire," and "execute."

By defining what it takes to lead at Standard Chartered, the agreement clearly defines the skills and actions associated with good leadership— balancing human or enabling skills with technical skills—which are also firmly linked to the organization's valued behaviors (and hence not something that exists in abstract). Many of these skills are critical for leaders to effectively guide skills-powered agile cohorts that come together for defined durations to deliver specific outcomes versus the traditional skills of leading in a hierarchical organization. These skills (as captured in the leadership agreement) include aligning talent to an aspirational vision, making it safe for them to set ambitious goals, making bold decisions, enabling them to experiment and learn from successes as well as failures, building trust by asking for and listening to feedback, coaching and helping others grow, and valuing diversity of thought. Through the agreement, a leadership movement has emerged that is being led and further catalyzed by people leaders, as demonstrated by their pledge to the agreement on the company's internal website. Further, practices and skills are embedded in how leaders are inducted, developed, measured, and recognized.

Developing Leadership Skills

Anchored around the leadership agreement, it then refreshed and modernized its core leadership programs for three distinct groups—a "core leadership" program for first-line people leaders, a "leaders of leaders" program for people leaders who have other people leaders reporting to them, and an "enterprise leaders" program for select high potential individuals at senior levels. Certifications are being introduced into these programs to ensure that the same standards are applied to measuring the development of leadership skills as any other critical skill required to operate a global financial services organization, aiming to certify all people leaders in three years. Monthly global people leader calls provide a platform for a cross-section of leaders to share their experiences and best practices. In addition to providing an opportunity to engage leaders, these calls help create a community that can learn from each other. For example, as COVID-19 pandemic restrictions eased and both employees and people leaders shifted from primarily remote to hybrid work environments, these global calls became a popular platform for sharing experiences, allowing the cohort to learn together, and from each other, how to navigate many previously unknown situations and challenges.

One of the key focus areas when making these significant investments in developing people leaders has been to embed learning agility as a key requirement and discipline, co-opting these leaders into building a strong learning culture among the teams they guide. By experiencing skill building themselves through different channels, formats, and platforms, leaders are becoming more confident in encouraging and directing their teams to leverage relevant developmental opportunities (i.e., building learning into the flow of work), and are learning how to increasingly incorporate skills into their day-to-day language. As they build their own skills to lead a high-performance organization, they are also learning how to coach their teams to help them navigate their careers in line with their aspirations and individual skills, further driving the development of a skills-powered enterprise.

This people leadership cohort is actively involved in shaping the company's overall strategic direction and cocreating key strategies and initiatives. Their role is incredibly important in the transition to becoming a more skills-powered enterprise, where leaders are becoming increasingly comfortable working with their HR business partners to challenge themselves to deconstruct jobs into tasks, enabling the underlying skills to be crowdsourced from across the firm. Such efforts have the potential for them to become the flag bearers for the shift toward "talent sharing" (versus "talent hoarding"), which is critical for skills to flow freely to where they are needed most.

At the same time there is awareness that as organizations evolve, the need for good leadership is not confined to people leader roles. Increasingly, there are a range of roles (e.g., product owners, squad leads, individual specialists) and ways of working (e.g., agile, self-directed teams) that require leadership beyond positional authority and line management. The leadership development program continues to evolve to encompass all aspects of leadership, aiming to cultivate this skill more broadly across the firm. This is done by democratizing access to leadership skill building through content-led, experiential, and community-based learning opportunities beyond the typical programmatic learning approach. It also offers an AI-enabled learning platform, called diSCover, where employees can access the leadership academy and use it at their own pace and preference. They can also sign up for a leadership health journey that delivers regular, bite-sized microlearning over sixty days, allowing them to build their leadership muscle through simple and practical "missions" focused on enabling performance, empowering people, driving vision, and continuing self-growth.

Measuring Leadership

While Standard Chartered has been measuring manager net promoter scores through its annual employee engagement survey for many years, it wanted to build a more holistic measurement that could help its people leaders better understand their impact, strengths, and areas of development. To do this, they designed and rolled out a leadership dashboard, which benchmarks leaders on the environment they create (using multiple data points from the annual employee engagement survey) and their leadership skills (leveraging data from their annual 360-degree feedback report). These insights are made available to the people leader and their own people leader to enable a constructive, balanced, and data-led dialogue. It enables the organization to understand its baseline skill levels for people leaders and drive better action planning. Additionally, it helps people leaders understand the importance of baselining skills within their own teams, which will be a critical enabler for establishing skills passports for employees.

Through this three-pronged approach of define, develop, and measure, there is increasing transparency and engagement with people leaders on what's expected of them as the nature of work and workforce expectations evolve, how they can develop themselves toward this standard, and what data they can leverage to ensure they are headed in the right direction. Equally important in this journey has been meaningful recognition of exemplary leadership, similar to how superlative performance is recognized. A new category for people leadership was instituted in the enterprise-wide recognition awards program that is overseen by the chairman. It is a strong signal of the importance placed by the global management team on this cohort, their skills, and their critical role in driving exponential impact and transformation.

2 The Reinvention of the Legacy Jobs–Based Organization as a Skills-Powered Organization

In their book *Reinventing the Organization*, Arthur Yeung and Dave Ulrich lay down the challenge for faster, more agile, and adaptive organizations.[1] They build the case for the perpetual reinvention of the organization by looking outward, becoming more market oriented, and emphasizing agility. They also emphasize the need for building, buying, and borrowing the capabilities you need to ensure an agile and adaptive organization. As we discuss in this chapter, the skills-powered organization can potentially deliver the exponential value gains that Yeung and Ulrich envision.

The following table depicts the three primary shifts we see as we evolve from the traditional jobs-based organization to a skills-powered one:

From	To
• Fixed structures	• Flexible constructs to optimize talent and technology
• Fixed jobs	• Fluid matching of skills/capabilities to work
• Own all capabilities	• Ecosystem of built, shared, and rented capabilities

The Star Model of Organization Design

There are many frameworks, each with its advantages and disadvantages. We find the star model of organization design to be most compelling and relevant. This framework can help describe the organizational implications of work-automation optimization. The star model was formulated by Jay Galbraith and refined by thinkers such as Amy Kates, Greg Kessler, Susan Mohrman, Christopher Worley, Edward Lawler, and Stu Winby. Galbraith described the model this way:

- Strategy: The strategy specifically delineates the products or services to be provided, the markets to be served, and the value offered to the customer. It also specifies sources of competitive advantage or capabilities.

- Structure: The organization's structure determines the placement of power and authority in the organization.

- Processes: Information and decision processes cut across the organization's structure; if we think of structure as the anatomy of the organization, processes are its physiology or functioning.

- Rewards: The purpose of the reward system is to align the employee's goals with the organization's goals. It provides motivation and incentive for completing the strategic direction.

- People practices: HR policies—in the appropriate combinations—produce the talent required by the organization's strategy and structure, generating the skills and mindsets necessary to implement the chosen direction.

Galbraith could hardly have imagined the recent advances in work and automation. The star model was developed and typically applied to traditional organizations and work done in traditional jobs through employment relationships. However, these organizational elements can also apply to the skills-powered organization. As Ravin Jesuthasan and John Boudreau describe in *Work without Jobs*, deconstructed and decoupled work changes the very definition of fundamental ideas such as capabilities, structure, processes, metrics, and HR practices. Their framework in the book suggests that "structure" and "process" are made up of increasingly deconstructed and decoupled tasks (and the underlying skills) that are constantly reinvented and optimized to account for automation, as well as alternative work arrangements such as gigs, contracts, projects, and tours of duty. It means that work and organizations are constantly evolving and being reinvented.

In *Work without Jobs*, Jesuthasan and Boudreau explored the organization's evolution across these three dimensions through three models for organizing and connecting talent to work.[2] Figure 2.1 depicts these three models and some of their core underpinning constructs.

Let's start on the left with the fixed model. With the job as its core underpinning, this construct was developed for the increasingly complicated but relatively stable world of the late nineteenth century/early twentieth century. The jobs are aggregated into job families, job families aggregated into functions, and functions combined into that more traditional hierarchical structure we are all familiar with. The primary organizational imperatives that underpin this construct are a focus on increasing scale (to offset the

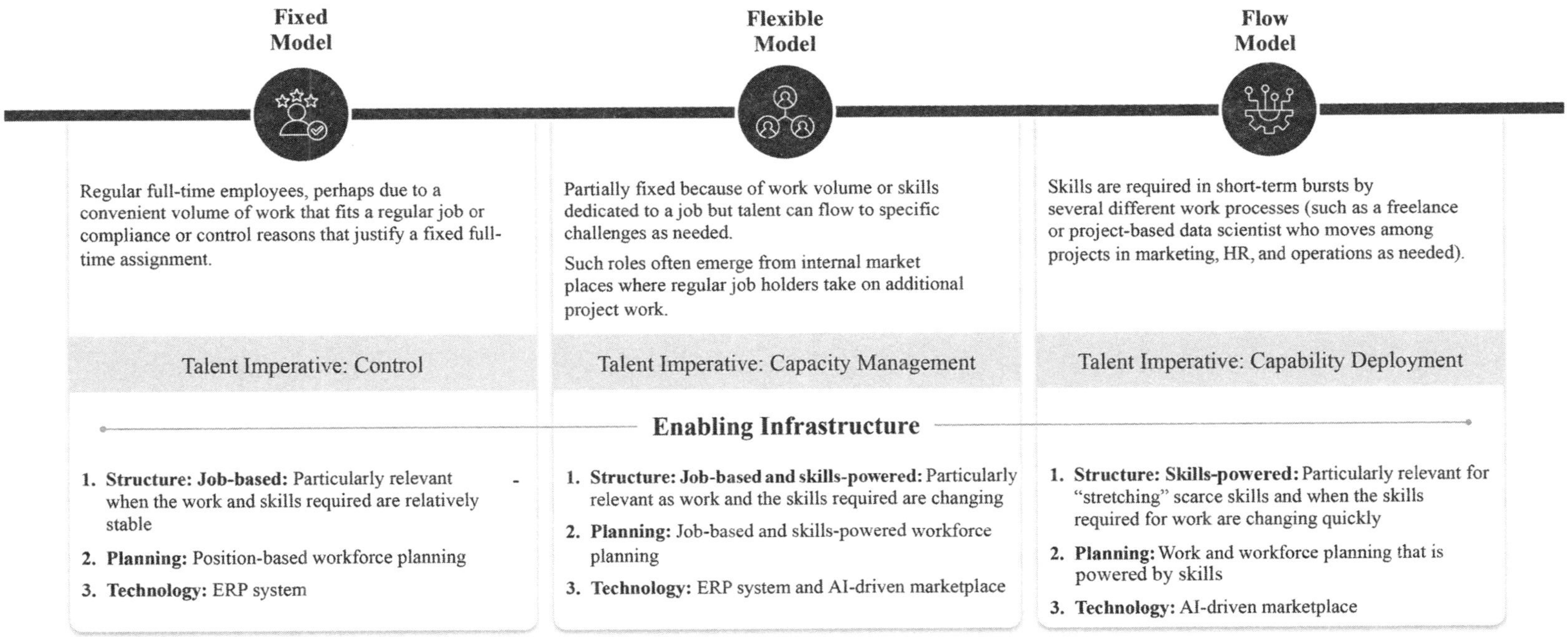

Fixed Model	Flexible Model	Flow Model
Regular full-time employees, perhaps due to a convenient volume of work that fits a regular job or compliance or control reasons that justify a fixed full-time assignment.	Partially fixed because of work volume or skills dedicated to a job but talent can flow to specific challenges as needed. Such roles often emerge from internal market places where regular job holders take on additional project work.	Skills are required in short-term bursts by several different work processes (such as a freelance or project-based data scientist who moves among projects in marketing, HR, and operations as needed).
Talent Imperative: Control	Talent Imperative: Capacity Management	Talent Imperative: Capability Deployment

Enabling Infrastructure

Fixed Model:
1. **Structure: Job-based:** Particularly relevant when the work and skills required are relatively stable
2. **Planning:** Position-based workforce planning
3. **Technology:** ERP system

Flexible Model:
1. **Structure: Job-based and skills-powered:** Particularly relevant as work and the skills required are changing
2. **Planning:** Job-based and skills-powered workforce planning
3. **Technology:** ERP system and AI-driven marketplace

Flow Model:
1. **Structure: Skills-powered:** Particularly relevant for "stretching" scarce skills and when the skills required for work are changing quickly
2. **Planning:** Work and workforce planning that is powered by skills
3. **Technology:** AI-driven marketplace

Figure 2.1

Enabling the skills-powered enterprise. *Source:* Ravin Jesuthasan and John Boudreau. Adapted from Ravin Jesuthasan and John Boudreau, "Work without Jobs," *Sloan Management Review,* January 5, 2021.

high fixed cost of building and owning all the capabilities needed to operate), driving efficiency (to lower said fixed cost), and placing a premium on expertise to increase the value of inputs. In this model, with its primary talent imperative of control to maximize the predictability with which inputs are converted into outputs, the job is the logical building block given the full and permanent focus of the jobholder on the tasks comprising the job.

While the shift in the world of work is certainly toward the flexible and flow models, the fixed model continues to be relevant, particularly for work where there is a premium on compliance or control (think quality control or piloting an airplane). The infrastructure underpinning this fixed model includes job architectures that allow talent to move from one job to another as demand for work evolves, planning denominated by jobholders moving within and across job families, and technology infrastructure mostly comprising enterprise resource planning (ERP) systems that support data management as talent is acquired, developed, deployed and transitioned.

Now let's turn our attention to the flexible model. This more recent phenomenon is built for an increasingly complex world characterized by growing uncertainty, volatility in demand and supply, and a changing set of requirements of both the organization of talent and vice versa. The structure here is a hybrid of a traditional hierarchy, combined with the flexibility for talent to be deployed and redeployed at speed as demand changes. The primary organizational imperatives underpinning this model are a growing premium on speed, agility, and flexibility. Unlike the emphasis on expertise to increase the quality of inputs in the fixed model, there is a growing focus on execution as the aforementioned external factors reduce the timeframe within which value can be captured.

In this model, the talent imperative shifts from control to managing capacity across the organization. We begin to see the emergence of the hybrid state where jobs and skills are the currency of work. Talent might still be in jobs, but they have the flexibility to either express their skills in different domains (e.g., a data scientist from IT who takes on a workforce analytics project in HR) or acquire new skills that align with their passions and interests (e.g., a finance professional who volunteers for a DEI project) through projects and assignments. The infrastructure underpinning this flexible model includes a hybrid construct that combines job architectures and skills-powered constructs powered by robust skill taxonomies. Planning is a mix of job-based and skills-powered planning as jobs coexist with projects, assignments, and gigs. The technology infrastructure combines ERP systems with internal talent marketplaces (something we will explore in much detail in chapter 5) that use AI to match the demand for work with the supply of skills and provides insights into the skill gaps needing to be closed.

The flow model is the third model, driven by the need to navigate an external environment characterized by volatility, hypercompetition, and high uncertainty. The primary organizational imperatives underpinning the flexible model of speed, agility, and flexibility are dialed to eleven in this scenario. Talent connects to work through projects, assignments, and gigs, as AI continuously monitors the changing demand for work, infers the skills required, and matches talent to work. The talent imperative in this scenario is one of capability deployment as skills become the pure currency of work.

The flow model enables the organization to more seamlessly access capabilities that are built (employees), shared (third-party talent), and rented (gig workers) based on the matching of their skills to work. The infrastructure includes a skill taxonomy continuously updated as demand for work evolves. Work and workforce planning are denominated by the skills required and supplied as each individual is viewed as a unique bundle of skills that is continuously evolving (rather than a jobholder who is defined by their current job). The underlying technology is a series of skills-powered platforms that offer visibility into the internal and external supply of skills, enable continuous matching of skills to work, and provide learning resources to talent. This approach is particularly effective as it directs resources where skill gaps are identified, based on mismatches between the evolving demands of work and the supply of skills across the workforce. In this model, talent is organized into squads that come together to take on various projects and tribes that are more enduring communities that learn, grow, and develop together.

As AI continues to reinvent work—substituting some activities, augmenting others, and transforming yet others—the required skills will change at increasing speed. Some skills will be rendered obsolete, others will change in their application as AI and automation increasingly augment them, and new ones will be demanded. Organizations (and talent) will only stay relevant if they can upskill and reskill at the pace of AI as the half-life of many skills shrinks dramatically and new ones emerge. Recall the infamous words of Alvin Toffler that we cited in the last chapter: "The illiterate of the 21st century will not be those who cannot read and write, but those who cannot learn, unlearn, and relearn." We will now explore the flow model, as it represents the most radical shift from the current state of work, through its application at a global insurance company. The analysis of the skills-powered fixed and flexible models will be addressed in the Standard Chartered case study later in this chapter.

The Flow Model in Action at a Global Insurance Company

In *Work without Jobs*, Jesuthasan and Boudreau described the flow model in action at a global insurance company.[3] Let's revisit that example and explore how it has evolved since.

A global insurer created an agile, global shared data science capability supporting its worldwide functions and divisions, extracting all such talent from their jobs within other parts of the organization. The intent was to enable talent to flow to projects through the matching of skills to work instead of the legacy approach of matching a person to a position. The insurer first defined all the skills required in a data science function (e.g., knowledge and ability to use programming languages such as R and Python, knowledge of linear modeling). All talent was assigned to a single job code in the company's system of record, and a baseline for compensation was established. Actual pay levels were then flexed up or down from that baseline based on the market price of various combinations of skills possessed by the talent (e.g., someone with Python, R, and linear modeling skills versus someone else with Python, R, and Angular skills). The talent was managed as pools of skills and matched to a variety of types of work (projects, assignments, etc.).

A new HR center of expertise helped business leaders design projects and assignments instead of opening a requisition for a new job as they would have done in the past. These projects were posted on the company's global internal talent marketplace, and the machine learning algorithm underpinning the marketplace translated the work activities within each project into the skills required to perform the work. The algorithm then matched the required skills with those of the talent in the shared data science function. It also considered where talent may have adjacent skills to do the work, their interest in it, and their capacity to take it on. The algorithm also analyzed the diversity of talent pools for different skill sets to ensure that work and development opportunities were being extended to talent in a way that would consistently increase the diversity of each talent pool.

Last, the algorithm also sent signals to employees as to what skills were trending up versus trending down in the marketplace, along with specific upskilling recommendations so talent could continue to stay relevant in the face of the organization's evolving work. To ensure that talent was sufficiently motivated to keep upskilling and reskilling themselves, the organization instituted a skills-powered pay structure with varying skill premiums, based on the value of different skills to the organization, applied to a baseline salary. Successful execution of projects was recognized through a project-based bonus pool shared by everyone who contributed to the project.

The cultural and capability shift required of managers to operate in this way is significant. The perceived loss of control and complexity that comes from having to get work done through the assignments and projects that underpin the flow model, and not through their own full-time employees in fixed jobs, required the organization to engage in some intensive change management. The change management plan included compiling resources to help managers understand the economic rationale for this model, providing support for constructing and designing projects, and clearly defining outcomes for work done in assignments and projects. For example, to ensure that everyone working on a project, whether they were in Mumbai or San Francisco, was equally engaged and collaborating effectively, managers were asked to ensure that everyone participated in virtual meetings. They did not meet in a conference room as this had the effect of creating an "uneven playing field" and inhibiting full and equal participation, particularly in highly collaborative activities.

A sort of career progression evolved in this skills-driven flow model, based on acquiring higher-order or higher-demand skills (as opposed to moving up from one job level to another). The company identified high-demand skills not only as those demanded inside the insurer's organization but also through using data from external organizations like Lightcast to provide insight into the external demand for various skills. These two sources of data were combined to inform the data science workers about the skills they should acquire to stay relevant to current and likely future projects. The work platform's algorithms also calculated gaps between the skills offered by workers and the skills needed by the posted projects. These skill gaps were matched to learning resources, which were recommended to "almost qualified" candidates to make themselves fully qualified.

This insurer's data science function illustrates the power and potential of the flow model. While the workers were all initially company employees (the organization subsequently opened the model to gig talent), they are not organized into jobs. They instead continually flow to assignments and projects. A key foundation for this ecosystem is that the workers are not seen as jobholders but rather as bundles of deconstructed skills/capabilities who are available for assignments and can be augmented as gaps are revealed. Workers are now treated as a more complete skill profile rather than only as jobholders, and careers can be more fluid because they are not limited by whether there is an available "next job." The impact of this shift from a fixed to a flow model was a 600 percent gain in the data scientists' productivity. This was the result of the following factors:

- Greater agility in deploying talent to where it is needed most across the company (one of the primary benefits of the flow model)
- Lower turnover (on account of a greater diversity of projects and access to continuous developmental opportunities across the company)
- Greater engagement (due to the skills-powered pay program and developmental opportunities)
- Reduced downtime (as the organization could be more planful in matching demand signals to the supply and availability of skills)

A Description of the Structure of a Skills-Powered Organization

We thought it would be interesting to ask ChatGPT, our now ubiquitous source for all knowledge, about the structure of a skills-powered organization. Here is what it had to say:

A skills-powered organization is structured around the expertise and capabilities of its employees rather than traditional hierarchical roles or job titles. In this type of organization, the focus is on identifying and leveraging the skills and strengths of individual employees to achieve organizational goals. Here are some characteristics of a skills-powered organization:

1. Fluid and adaptable roles: In a skills-powered organization, roles are not fixed or limited by job descriptions. Employees are encouraged to develop and use their skills across projects and initiatives. They may have primary areas of

expertise but are also given opportunities to contribute in other areas where their skills are valuable.

2. Skill identification and mapping: The organization invests in identifying and documenting the skills of its employees. This involves assessing individual strengths, capabilities, and interests through various methods such as self-assessments, performance evaluations, and feedback from peers and supervisors. The organization may use tools or software to map and categorize these skills for easy access and use.

3. Skills-powered teams and projects: Instead of forming teams based on traditional departments or job functions, skills-powered organizations create teams and projects based on the required skills for a specific task or objective. The organization identifies the necessary skill sets and assembles a team of individuals with the right expertise to achieve the desired outcomes. This allows for flexibility in team formation and promotes collaboration and knowledge sharing.

4. Continuous learning and development: Skills-powered organizations prioritize learning and development initiatives to enhance employees' existing skills and help them acquire new ones. They provide opportunities for training, workshops, mentorship, and access to resources that enable employees to stay updated and grow professionally. This emphasis on continuous learning helps the organization adapt to changing industry landscapes and remain competitive.

5. Agile decision-making and problem-solving: In a skills-powered organization, decision-making and problem-solving are decentralized to empower employees at all levels. Since individuals are selected for teams based on their skills and expertise, they have the knowledge and autonomy to contribute to decision-making processes. This agility allows the organization to respond quickly to challenges and take advantage of opportunities.

6. Collaboration and knowledge sharing: Skills-powered organizations foster a culture of collaboration and knowledge sharing. Employees are encouraged to work together, leveraging their respective skills and experiences to solve problems and innovate. Knowledge-sharing platforms, regular meetings, and open communication channels facilitate the exchange of ideas and expertise throughout the organization.

7. Performance measurement based on skills: Rather than evaluating employees solely based on job titles or rigid performance metrics, skills-powered organizations assess performance based on the skills and contributions individuals bring to the organization. This approach encourages employees to focus on skill development and applying their expertise in meaningful ways.

Overall, a skills-powered organization recognizes and values its employees' diverse skills and talents. By leveraging these skills effectively, such organizations can create a dynamic, collaborative, and agile work environment that fosters innovation, adaptability, and growth.

This is a compelling vision and a robust description of a skills-powered organization! Interestingly, these dimensions are all reflected in the flow model as illustrated by the insurance company case study we just reviewed.

Let's turn our attention to Standard Chartered and explore how it has, and continues to, evolve on its journey to becoming a skills-powered organization. Specifically, we will discuss how it has adapted the fixed model of work and introduced the flexible model to make skills the currency of work.

Shifting the Narrative from "Jobs" to "Skills" at Standard Chartered

Letting go of the paradigm of jobs, organizational levels, and structures that have been the norm, especially for a large, multimarket enterprise over a hundred years old, can be a mammoth (and potentially overwhelming) task. The HR team at Standard Chartered thus consciously started their journey with the concept of jobs as the currency of work (the fixed model) while shifting the narrative to skills. Recognizing that they had to strike a conscious balance between experimenting in pockets and making change happen at scale, they started by introducing a strategic workforce planning process (an analysis that is now refreshed on an annual basis), which showed business leaders the nature and volume of jobs that were expected to decrease or no longer be relevant over the next three to five years and the ones expected to increase or be created during the same period. The former category is referred to as sunset roles and includes roles in operations, sales support, and administration. The latter category is called sunrise roles and includes jobs in cloud engineering, cybersecurity, UX design, and change management.

Embedding this approach to workforce planning required significant change management, especially in building leadership insight and understanding how business transformation directly impacts demand for skills and the roles they underpin at a granular level. Extensive external research on technology, market, and customer trends supported internal insights on workforce demand and supply (including attrition rates and workforce composition by job family and skill levels). These were critical to estimating not just the future size and shape of the organization but also the nature and quantum of future skills required and the gap between the current and future target state. This analysis became a starting point for HR leadership to drive a discussion on buy versus build with the business and the economic impact of decisions around hiring externally versus reskilling and deploying internally.

The SWP was a critical starting point, both because it created an incredibly tangible commercial case for the board and senior management and brought to the fore how the changing demand for skills would have a far-reaching impact on the firm. It showed that junior roles were expected to be displaced disproportionately, shifting the organization's shape from a pyramid to a diamond, with significant cost implications. This also allowed it to understand the implications for the diversity of its workforce. The analysis highlighted that the proportion of women in its workforce would shrink by almost 2 percentage points due to the high number of women employed in sunset roles, with many of the sunrise roles currently being more male dominated. This led to deliberate action being taken to minimize this risk.

The sunrise and sunset roles linked with the competency frameworks also provided insights on the growing and declining skills associated with these roles. However, without live data on the skills held, both at an organizational and individual level, the picture being painted was based on a "static," almost top-down view of the skills required for each role (versus a ground-up view centered on a skills taxonomy). The HR team knew that this was not ideal but was conscious of the need to make a start to initiate the narrative around skills and then iterate to drive progress.

Building on the SWP, Standard Chartered then began building a self-sustaining learning habit and pivoting its focus toward developing the skills underpinning the sunrise roles (such as the future skills academies and POC experiments we discuss in chapter 3). It was important to establish a common language centered around skills by seeding the concept into the day-to-day narrative of employees and people leaders, beginning with learning, development, and career growth at an individual level while showing them the business and client impact. This enabled HR to start shifting the conversation away from the one-to-one relationship between people and jobs—something they were comfortable with—to the many-to-many between skills and work, which was a somewhat novel concept to many but pivotal to enabling the redeployment of talent that the SWP had highlighted. Active partnership between the HR and business teams became critical for cocreating and leading on the skills agenda. So too was building strong senior sponsorship so that business leaders were investing the time to understand the opportunities available for upskilling and reskilling and talking to their teams about it. This partnership has been essential for encouraging people leaders to move from a talent-hoarding to a talent-sharing mindset to eventually enable skills to flow across the firm, from sunset work to sunrise work.

Since this work was initiated, Standard Chartered has been pushing beyond previous boundaries to build the organizational capabilities and drive the shift needed, not just to enhance the identification and development of future-focused skills but also to get better at rapidly locating these skills and deploying them to the areas of greatest impact, at speed and scale, agnostic of where the skills reside within the organization. In chapters 3 and 5, we will delve further into how it is breaking down silos and hierarchies and introducing work methods that support a democratized working environment (the flex and flow models) that enable multidisciplinary teams to quickly connect and execute on specific priorities. Using a virtual AI-driven internal talent marketplace, underused skills are being unleashed beyond the rigid scope of job structures to unlock the capacity and ambition of its workforce to a fuller extent in service of client needs and business outcomes. As employees and people leaders increasingly engage with the internal talent marketplace, the shift is visible in how they are thinking about the work that needs to be delivered—deconstructing jobs into tasks and activities and then "crowdsourcing" the underlying skills required to execute the tasks from various parts of the organization.

As it continues to embed this flexible way of working to enhance productivity and more efficiently and effectively deploy the skills needed to execute various strategic priorities, Standard Chartered is also exploring pockets where it might experiment with a flow model. These include areas where it has been creating agile teams around specific products and digital priorities, as well as some of its entrepreneurial ventures where it has seen how the flow model is helping it better respond to customer needs at speed. One opportunity being considered is in its technology vertical, where it is looking at how it might design and deploy a pilot to transition its engineering teams to a skills-powered flow model. This could allow it to rapidly identify, assess, develop, and deploy talent based on specialized engineering skills, beginning the shift from jobs to skills as the currency of work.

3 The Skills-Powered Organization and the Work Experience

As you have seen throughout the preceding three chapters, the skills-powered organization redefines everything we think we know about organizing, leading, and managing work. It also materially transforms how work is experienced. This chapter will illustrate that work experience is changing. But before we delve into that, let's take a step back and understand the two primary anchors: reshaping work and the experience of work. Think back to the introduction and our retrospective on the evolution of work over the last 140 years and the expected changes over the next 20. As we explore what it will take for leaders to thrive in the "next of work" that is increasingly driven by the skills-powered organization, we see them needing to address two pivotal questions:

1. How will we redesign work to allow talent to flow to it as seamlessly as possible while enabling its perpetual reinvention as we increasingly seek to decouple growth from resource intensity?
2. How will we reenvision the work experience to meet all talent where they are and, on their terms, customize and personalize the experience similarly to the consumer experience, creating a more equitable, inclusive, and accountable culture?

Answering these two questions will require a dramatic and radical rethink of work and its experience. Let's explore each of these questions in greater detail.

Redesigning Work

As we increasingly move from fixed to flex to flow models of work to respond to the demand for a more resilient, agile, and flexible enterprise, we need to ensure that not only is talent being connected to work more seamlessly but also can remain relevant for the rapidly changing demand for work. This will be essential if we fundamentally alter the economics of work by decoupling growth from resource intensity. The shrinking half-life of skills has seen off the old days when we could ask our talent to take a course occasionally and reskill on their own time. The sheer quantum of upskilling and reskilling requires organizations to intentionally design a space for learning in the flow of work, where development is made a core part of the work experience and the talent value proposition. A large airline recently redefined its talent value proposition from its legacy "deal" that was indexed to stability of employment, flexible schedules, and flight benefits to one that put development and growth at the very heart of its proposition, which brought with it the promise of continued relevance for a changing world. In their words, "We will develop you for opportunity, either within or without."

Reskilling at an Oil and Gas Company

A major oil and gas company sought to reinvent its work for greater profitability while preserving the talent in the numerous small communities in which it operated. Through the introduction of performance drilling tools and integrated technology that was both developed internally and acquired, the company transformed its rigs into a platform for multiple services. It moved to a 24/7 centrally controlled operations center to manage the performance of its oil rigs. The company made the following shifts to its work:

From	To
• Analog gauges and operator expertise	• Digital, interactive "cockpits" with automated functions
• Primarily physical work	• Primarily mental work augmented with automation
• High labor intensity and low skill requirements	• Lower labor intensity and higher skill requirements
• Significant variation in operating performance and predictability of maintenance	• Greater predictability of maintenance events and much lower performance variation through sensors, AI, and analytics

As it reinvented its work, the organization upskilled and reskilled all its talent to take on higher value-added work. The impact of the transformation was an improvement in profitability per rig of 45 percent despite wage premiums increasing between 7 and 13 percent due to the higher skill requirements. Figure 3.1 illustrates the shifting skill requirements of its motorhands who were reskilled into the newly created role of rig technician. Beyond the immediate impact of this work reinvention and upskilling and reskilling, the organization set the stage for its perpetual reinvention in the face of advancing technology by creating the mindset and conditions to engage its talent in their continuous upskilling and reskilling.

We will explore the design of work and the development and deployment of talent in more detail in chapter 4, as it is one of the core capabilities of the skills-powered organization.

Reenvisioning the Work Experience

As we have discussed previously, the essence of the work experience underpinning the skills-powered organization is the shift from the one-to-one relationship between jobholders in jobs matched to linear career paths to the many-to-many relationships between skills and work with talent matched to many different types of work experiences based on the skills required for work (demand) and the skills and interests of the person (supply). As Ravin Jesuthasan and John Boudreau described in *Work without Jobs*, the disruptions of the COVID-19 pandemic (accelerating virtual work for many workers and organizations) and global social justice movements caused organizations to rethink work and their relationships with all sorts of workers, including employees, contractors, and retirees.[1] One question is how to better ensure worker well-being; one answer is to add flexibility, allowing more personalized worker engagement with the organization. At the extreme, each worker might choose where, when, and how they work as well as the terms and conditions of their work (i.e., meeting each person on their terms).

Some describe this as a human-centric organization that shapes to fit talent versus shaping talent to fit the organization. This idea is consistently invoked in emerging ideas, including the "reinvented organization,"[2] "holacracy,"[3] and "humanocracy."[4] Such human-centric approaches require a

Motorhand (current state)

- Routinely check engine equipment, complete reading sheets, and report problems
- Perform routine engine testing and maintenance
- Complete routine paperwork
- Maintain and repair engine and fuel systems

Key Job Activities

- Pick up and lay down pipe or casing
- Rig up wire line machine and run survey
- Line up trip tank, prepare for hole fill, and read or gauge trip tank volume
- Add/remove a generator from the system
- Check the coolant level and add fluid to the radiator of an engine
- Clean electrical houses and surrounding area
- Install grounding
- Maintain a parts inventory
- Perform a complete check of all fluid levels on an engine
- Perform preventative maintenance on an air compressor
- Pressure up/down accumulator and perform routine maintenance

Legacy Skills:
- Specialized knowledge of engine and fueling systems
- Foundational electrical knowledge
- Working within defined procedures

Skills

Figure 3.1
Reskilling talent at an oil and gas company

foundation of the new work operating system based on deconstruction. The traditional system of jobs and jobholders is incapable of such personalization and is far less agile than needed to respond to changing organization and worker needs and preferences.

Human-Centric Work Reinvention at a Global Pharmaceutical Company

A global pharmaceutical company illustrates the power of the skills-powered organization. Even before the 2020 pandemic, it had already established flexible work policies to allow some employees to work from home, introducing diversity and inclusion programs to support an inclusive culture. However, the pandemic and social justice movements of 2020 revealed that much more

Rig Technician (future state)

- Routinely check engine equipment, complete reading sheets, and report problems
- Perform routine engine testing and maintenance
- Complete routine paperwork
- Maintain and repair engine and fuel systems

- Communicate with the District Operations Supervisors for issues that cannot be resolved via phone and/or email
- Resolve problems by clarifying issues through researching and exploring solutions, and by escalating unresolved problems
- Complete preventive maintenance work orders according to system requirements and close them out in the system
- Troubleshoot transducers, cat 5/fiber optic cabling
- Service and repair communication systems
- Maintenance/repair of rig air system
- Run diagnostic testing on electrical equipment
- Maintain hydraulic power units (hydraulic hoists, automated floor wrenches, and automated catwalk)

Emerging Skills:
- Advanced electrical and mechanical knowledge, to perform both preventative maintenance and complex repairs on a wide range of rig equipment
- Enhanced communications and collaboration skills
- Decision-making skills
- Complex problem-solving skills

could be done to achieve the goals of being a more flexible and equitable workplace.[5]

Let's explore some of these changes and the perpetual evolution enabled by its shift to a work operating system powered by skills:

Schedules and locations are flexible. The organization had offered limited flexibility, including remote work limited to three days a month from home, no employees outside of the organization's main campuses, and all employees to be "present" between 9:00 a.m. and 5:00 p.m. It aspired to have more flexibility, such as unlimited work from home, employees located anywhere in the United States, and any work schedule as long as it included forty hours per week and met productivity goals.

How does being a skills-powered organization support such aspirations? How would the company equitably compensate talent in different locations performing the same work? The solution was to determine salaries based on the market value for skills while applying a geographic differential to reflect the different local living costs. By determining the market value of skills instead of jobs, the company was able to "personalize" compensation by recognizing unique skill combinations that might typically have been obscured when they are embedded in the market price for a single job or might not typically be available because they didn't fit any of the existing job descriptions.

Flexibility is extended to lab and manufacturing jobs. Before 2020, flexible work (e.g., choosing where to live, working from home or local office facilities, and sharing work with colleagues across locations) had been available only in white-collar jobs. The company aspired to expand that flexibility to lab and manufacturing jobs (e.g., workers could choose their residence cities, lab workers could work in leased lab facilities at local universities, and manufacturing workers could gain flexibility through shift sharing, shift swapping, or short shifts). The skills-powered work operating system ensured no decline in manufacturing productivity with such flexibility. An algorithm worked at the task level to integrate production requirements with requested worker flexibility arrangements, calculate each worker's optimum schedule, and recommend whether supervisors should approve, modify, or deny each worker's request.

Flexible work arrangements offer more options and can be changed. In the old system, work relationships were limited to full- or part-time employees or independent contractors, and no movement was allowed between each category. The aspiration was to offer more options (temporary, job sharing, freelancing, gigs, etc.) and make moving between categories easier. For example, full-time employees might temporarily move to a part-time job share, or retirees could take on gig projects and shift to fixed-term contracts. This increased flexibility required a new approach to work planning. It also required planning talent requirements at the task and skill level and using data-based triggers to predict change requests in work engagements. Simulation modeling predicted the impact of different potential work arrangements on organizational performance and productivity.

A culture of inclusion extends beyond the walls of the organization. The racial justice movement in the United States prompted much soul-searching in the organization as it considered both its own culture and its impact on the communities in which it operated. As it questioned every aspect of its legacy, the organization looked at both these issues through the eyes of its minority employees and candidates and the marginalized members of its communities. How could this new approach to flexible work contribute? The skills-powered operating model allowed the company to become more attractive to a more diverse population of skilled talent who were not well represented in some of its operating locations. The new flexible work design and arrangements were often more compatible with this talent pool than relying on the old system of intact jobs. As these new, diverse workers joined the organization, it became apparent that other changes could make the organization more inclusive. The organization developed new continual listening processes to ensure that the more inclusive group of workers' voices were reflected in its code of conduct and values. It committed to making every worker responsible for consistently living and practicing organizational values.

Social upheaval creates opportunities that exceed the capabilities of the traditional work operating system. The skills-powered organization offers a better platform to address evolving productivity challenges and opportunities and the increasing environmental, social, and governance challenges from the external context by continually recalibrating work and the organization.

A skills-powered organization creates many of the necessary conditions for talent from various diverse backgrounds to engage with work on their terms, increasing equity and inclusion. Let's now explore the work experience at Standard Chartered and how it made growth and development central to its EVP while driving DEI.

The Work Experience at Standard Chartered

The opportunity at hand for Standard Chartered was very clear. In 2018, it undertook a piece of research to identify the core factors underpinning the EVP for both current and potential employees—"career opportunities" and "development opportunities" were among the top six talent attraction factors and deemed to be two of the four most differentiating EVP attributes. However, these were also some of the lowest-scoring items in the annual employee engagement survey every year as well as in exit surveys. As the team delved further into these two topics, it became clear that one of the drivers of this sentiment was a strong belief among employees that career growth within the organization could only be achieved through vertical movement. This was a challenge as vertical progression (i.e., grade promotions) cannot happen as frequently, or for as many people as employees want, due to the significant pressure it places on any company's operating model and cost structure. There was, therefore, a compelling need to both shift the perception of employees and enhance their experience, demonstrating that career development is as much about becoming future ready as it is about an individual's next role.

To make this happen, the leadership team knew it would be critical to build a strong learning culture across the firm. They knew that while they could set up all the systems and provide all the necessary tools and learning content, employees needed to be onboard with the urgent need to upskill and reskill and take ownership of their learning. This also meant expanding beyond the traditional approach of training people to improve their performance in their current role and preparing them for their next role. The shift included taking a huge leap forward toward helping employees build the specific skills the organization required for the future (as determined by the sunrise roles identified through its SWP) as well as role-agnostic skills that would keep them relevant and employable more broadly.

For example, while expanding the skill sets of relationship managers (RMs) in their current jobs (i.e., role-based learning), the leadership also recognized the necessity to invest in learning journeys. These journeys would enable tellers and other frontline staff in branches to reskill and become universal bankers, also known as mini-RMs (i.e., role-to-role reskilling). Additionally, there was a focus on developing systemic skills such as digital and data analysis for all employees. The need to pivot to a more skills-powered approach became critical, entailing a balance between the expectations of its employees and the capabilities Standard Chartered needs to stay ahead of the evolving customer demand and competition.

In 2019, it embarked on this journey by doing the "definitional" work of identifying the skills needed for the future of banking. It launched a multiyear journey to revolutionize how people learn in the organization while helping the workforce build sustainable learning habits. Learning has since been made more democratic and personalized, establishing these as foundational principles of the developmental interventions it has deployed and continues to embed, with technology being a key enabler.

The internal learning experience platform—diSCover—that was introduced in mid-2020 started to shift the learning experience away from traditional classroom-based learning (face-to-face or virtual) to one where people can consume learning content in bite-sized chunks at their own pace and in their own space, including through a mobile app. Using AI, the platform can customize the user experience to the learning preferences of each individual. Future skills academies were then built on the platform to ensure that resources—whether budgets, the bandwidth of the learning and development team, or employee time—were directed toward the future of work and banking. This was accomplished through focusing on the development of specific technical skills (i.e., those essential to embracing disruptive technologies such as digital, data analysis and visualization, cybersecurity, and sustainable finance) and enabling or human skills (i.e., those that help us deliver what technology and machines cannot, such as managing ambiguity, critical thinking, innovation, entrepreneurship, creativity, leadership, emotional intelligence, and empathy).

While learning in the classroom is certainly not dead, instructor-led training has become increasingly focused on simulating real-world experiences and making learning more social rather than a means for delivering content. This has also meant the increasing use of innovative learning formats such as online brain-training games and virtual simulation exercises that enable employees to build and practice skills, often daily and at a time that suits their schedule. These formats are taking learning from being theory and concept focused to being experience focused and practice led while enabling the philosophical shift from "getting better at doing a job" to developing a wide range of skills. For example, employees are using brain-training games to practice how to spot "dirty" data sets (e.g., those that result in inaccurate outcomes from AI). Playing these games for a few minutes each day and a few days a week builds data science skills in a way that reading through pages of content or listening to hours of instructions could never have.

Another good example is "Equilibrium," an immersive and experiential simulation that has been conceptualized in-house. The simulation lets employees see the impact of decisions and actions on the planet, people, and the economy. It allows them to virtually step into several personas—a multinational enterprise, a city president, a sustainable start-up, and a family-owned business—and provides decision-making opportunities as each entity transforms toward a more sustainable and profitable future. Points are earned based on how well they balance people, planet, and profit as they "run" companies and cities, allowing them to explore various combinations of decisions. The simulation provides space for feedback on the decisions made and helps employees build skills and develop insights into how they can support clients as they make similar decisions. Even though these games and simulations are online, they retain the human experience as employees can come together to play in teams, either in the same physical room or virtually from across different parts of the organization.

One of the key insights from the strategic workforce planning process has been the potential "worsening" of the gender mix in the overall workforce due to particular job families seeing a decline or increase in work. Many of the learning formats and journeys have been designed to address this. For example, women are underrepresented in the firm and across the industry in sunrise roles, such as those relating to digital and data. So how can the number of hurdles be reduced for women who aspire to be in these fields but otherwise might shy away from sitting in male-dominated classrooms to build their skills? The flexibility—and often anonymity—afforded by online learning is a crucial part of the solution. Multiple online platform providers, such as Coursera and FutureLearn, saw an increase in the number of women signing up for courses in STEM topics, including tech and software development, during the pandemic.[6] While the debate may continue around whether women hold themselves to higher readiness standards when raising their hand for a next role,[7] recent research underscores that advancing in the workforce continues to be more difficult for them.[8] Standard Chartered has been focused on helping its women talent feel more ready to take on one of these sunrise roles by empowering them to learn and build skills in safe spaces and in a flexible way that works for them, in addition to providing other types of support needed to sustain their career journeys.

As it uses AI to democratize access to learning, particularly through its future-focused academies, it has also adopted an AI-driven approach to democratizing access to opportunities where people can put existing and newly acquired skills into practice through an internal talent marketplace. The marketplace serves as an avenue where employees can develop or practice skills by taking on projects (or "gigs"). The AI powering the platform allows people to connect their skills, experiences, interests, and aspirations to gigs and projects that they can sign up for (in addition to their day jobs) as well as access mentors who can help them grow. These could be cross-functional or even cross-geographical projects where they can spend up to eight hours a week, with the duration of projects ranging from a few weeks to several months.

Executed without any intermediaries or approvals, the gigs are open to all and do not require manager approval. This marketplace is inclusive since access to these gigs is based on individuals' skills and aspirations, irrespective of organizational hierarchies or talent classifications. Employees can sign up for a gig that is focused on an area in which they want to build certain skills, a part of the business in which they have an interest, or a role that presents them with an opportunity to further hone existing skills by expressing them in a different domain. For example, one of the employees from the supply chain team in Chennai signed up for a gig posted by a colleague from the consumer banking business in Singapore. The gig was focused on improving the efficiency with which net promoter score data received through customers on the mobile and online banking channels was categorized. The employee was able to put his programming and data visualization skills into practice and helped design and deploy a new tool for text mining. The result was that the retail banking business was able to move from a manual approach to categorization that took three hours to an automated process that took fifteen minutes, allowing them to draw insights and act on customer feedback in a timely manner.

In addition to developing technical and human skills by solving real business challenges, the internal talent marketplace is also helping employees broaden their personal networks across the firm. It was thus not surprising to see the remarkable response that the pilot launch of the marketplace in India received in 2020, even as the workforce was grappling with the COVID-19 pandemic. Over six thousand employees signed up and accessed 280 gig opportunities during the pilot's first year. In 2021, as the marketplace expanded to further markets, it attracted almost eleven thousand employees, and by the end of 2022, when most of the global rollout was complete, there were over nineteen thousand users in the it's "internal gig economy"—accelerating the move toward a skills-powered talent deployment approach beyond jobs.

In addition to executing various campaigns to encourage the adoption and usage of the marketplace, an important part of Standard Chartered's journey has been consolidating the experience for employees. As a first step, the marketplace has been integrated with diSCover so that as employees document the skills they aspire to build and the algorithm in the marketplace uses this data to match them with gigs (more about this in chapter 5), the algorithm also directs them to the relevant learning content on diSCover so they can further develop those skills. Further, as it is strengthening its feedback culture, including focusing on peer feedback, access to the firm's always-on feedback tool (Feedback365) has been enabled via the marketplace to encourage employees who have worked together on gigs through the marketplace to share constructive, developmental feedback.

This has resulted in a massive cultural shift for the workforce. By having personalized and democratized access to learning and developmental experiences, the organization has been making skill building far more inclusive since it's no longer about who you know or where you are based that determines your access to these experiences. These investments are also increasing the employability of the workforce—not just internally but externally—as employees can showcase their diSCover learning badges on their LinkedIn profiles. This increased visibility and marketability is translating into great engagement as evidenced in recent employee engagement surveys. In 2020, the pilot locations for the talent marketplace saw the biggest year-on-year increase in satisfaction with career and development opportunities in the it's annual employee survey. From 2019 to 2023, the firm has seen a jump of over 5 percentage points globally in employee satisfaction with career and development opportunities.

The ability to sign up for gigs has also enabled employees to engage with work that delivers the greatest impact for them and, in many cases, is aligned with their personal purpose. This is especially true post-COVID-19. As more and more people evaluate what's important to them, their ask from employers is shifting toward how work can fit their personal lives and purpose. The issues of where and when people work were the first to be brought to the fore by the pandemic, with flexible working becoming a basic expectation among employees today. The workforce is increasingly questioning "what work I do," "how I work," and "why I work." Employees who seek variety in their work invest their energies in it. They want to be able to connect it with their individual purpose, and they want to have a greater say in who they work with as well as how they work to deliver various outcomes. An internal gig-based construct (powered by the underlying skills needed to do the work) allows employees to gravitate toward the work they feel most passionately about, whether out of curiosity to learn and acquire skills or the opportunity to use their skills to make an impact. It begins with the opportunity to take on these gigs alongside their day job but quickly becomes an expectation that this empowering experience of being able to choose their work will be how they work and grow. With skills being the markers of an employee's expertise and ability to contribute, not their job titles, the marketplace makes employees feel unique and valued.

At an organizational level, while the conversation started with the concept of jobs—something that business leaders were more comfortable and well-versed with—over time, the narrative has begun to transition to one centered around skills. The SWP and the reskilling/upskilling journeys enabled it's global management team and board to see the clear economic link between employee career development and the harnessing of emerging trends in technology and data to keep the company relevant for a very different financial services world. There was also the very tangible opportunity to reduce recruitment and employment costs by improving internal redeployment in addition to being attractive to the best talent available on account of the significant developmental opportunities available within the firm. The HR team identified that there was the potential for significant cost savings by reskilling and redeploying employees internally—a fact corroborated by the UK's Financial Services Skills Commission's research that estimates reskilling can create cost savings of up to £49,000 per, employee compared to eliminating talent in sunset jobs and hiring external talent with the skills needed for sunrise jobs.[9] As a result of the various initiatives we have discussed here, Standard Chartered saw internal hiring rates rise to 41 percent in 2021 from a previous five-year average of 35 percent.

One of the interventions to facilitate targeted internal hiring is the POC experiments being designed and deployed, aimed at upskilling/reskilling employees to resource priority roles. The POCs focus on sunrise roles such as cybersecurity analyst, universal banker, cloud security engineer, and data translator. These roles align with a strategic priority for the organization, and the scale of demand will likely grow over time. They are also being used to experiment with reskilling journeys that include personalized developmental advice based on the participants' likely skills starting point, mentoring by someone with more experience in these areas, opportunities for on-the-job learning and job shadowing, and scenario-based digital simulations. Recruiters can then nudge hiring managers to consider candidates who might otherwise not be considered for these roles on account of not having the "right" education or "relevant" prior work experience but have scored well in the learning modules and assessments undertaken as part of the POC and thus show they have developed the relevant skills required to perform the role.

Moreover, the firm uses a data-led approach to identify potential "candidate pools" of employees for these POCs based on the skills adjacency between their current role and the skills needed for the POC role. These pools are being drawn almost entirely from sunset roles, where redundancies are more likely to occur over the next few years, to enable purposeful redeployment opportunities. This is helping to proactively prevent the expected worsening of gender representation in the long run (as was identified in the strategic workforce planning analysis discussed earlier) while giving women employees a safe space to develop and practice skills and in turn gain confidence in their readiness for moving into a new role.

For Standard Chartered, cocreating across stakeholders (business leaders, employees, the HR function, and external partners) has been critical in driving progress around it'sskills journey. The senior sponsorship by the board and global management team has been pivotal in encouraging leaders to invest time and effort into understanding the opportunities of becoming more skills powered and ensuring that the interventions eventually drive outcomes for both colleagues and clients. For example, starting in 2021, it began establishing learning councils (starting with a global learning council, and increasingly business and function councils), where a cross-functional set of senior business leaders partner with the HR team to define the learning priorities and investments for the organization and play an active role in driving interest in skill building and learning adoption. Similarly, each of the POC experiments have a business sponsor, whose active inputs not only help in designing a relevant upskilling/ reskilling journey for the participants but also ensures there is ongoing commitment in driving redeployment after the development journey. Building out a comprehensive communication and engagement strategy, especially for bringing together a connected narrative for individual employees, teams, and people leaders around the various interventions, has also been important (and especially for multimarket companies as products and solutions are activated in varying contexts).

While top-down sponsorship has been important for enabling progress toward making skills the currency of work at Standard Chartered, it has been the conscious design choices that place employees at the heart of various interventions that have been critical for truly driving change from the bottom-up. This includes the choice to not require people leader approval for employees to sign up to gigs on the talent marketplace, or the choice to involve an increasing number of people leaders in curating it's annual global learning week (which in 2023 saw employees invest sixty-three thousand hours in themselves across four days). It also includes the choice to enable more social learning (such as by creating competitions when teams from across the globe "play and learn" through online simulations). By democratizing access, the various platforms and interventions are challenging the typical assumptions around organizational hierarchy and creating the space for the shift to being skills powered to be an employee-led movement.

4 The New Organizational Capabilities Underpinning the Skills-Powered Organization

We have discussed why a skills-powered organization is needed for the new world of work, what it looks like, how work is organized within such an enterprise, and what the talent experience feels like. In this chapter, we turn to the pivotal capabilities required to successfully operate it. Based on our collective experiences of Tanuj having guided the journey at Standard Chartered, and Ravin having worked with numerous large and small organizations to help them become skills-powered organizations, we consistently see three organizational capabilities as being pivotal to delivering the workforce, cultural, and business outcomes of such an enterprise, as illustrated in figure 4.1. These capabilities are needed above and beyond the basic infrastructure of having a skills taxonomy to define and govern all the organization's skills.

The capability of work design is essential to understanding the true demand for skills and how they can best be connected to work. Talent development is pivotal to ensuring skills are acquired in a timely and efficient manner based on the demand signals from work design. Last, talent deployment is the critical capability of enabling the expression of the demanded skills across a variety of work engagements with optimal efficiency, effectiveness, and impact as defined in the introduction.

Each of these capabilities is underpinned by three key enablers: process, technology, and new rules for leadership. Or, as our friend and colleague Gary Bolles describes in his book *The Next Rules of Work*, the skill set, toolset, and mindset.[1] As we explore these three capabilities, it is worth noting that like any transformation, many other capabilities are required to sustain and embed change. These include managing the change, leadership skills and capabilities, and organization redesign. We will not be delving into

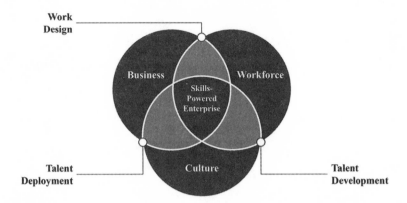

Figure 4.1
Core capabilities of the skills-powered enterprise

those more general capabilities that are prerequisites for success. Rather, we instead focus on the areas we view as being fundamental pivot points in this journey as they challenge some of the most common beliefs and rules that organizations and leaders operate by.

Work Design

For decades, leaders have responded to changing work requirements by hiring, firing, and redeploying jobholders in fixed roles. As they face a growing plurality of means for accomplishing work (think AI, robotics, gig talent, shared services, etc.) and there is an increasing demands for agility and flexibility in acquiring, deploying, and combining these methods, the need to redesign work at speed and scale while considering the associated costs, risks, and returns is becoming a critical requirement for all leaders. As we have described before, a skills-powered operating model is critical to enabling the optimal combinations of various AI/automation options and talent in a variety of organizing constructs (full-time employees, gig workers, talent in agile pools, third-party labor, etc.). In our experience, work design is becoming one of the most critical capabilities required of organizations to seamlessly match skills to rapidly evolving work. So, what does that look like?

The following process, initially described in *Work without Jobs*, is one that we have found to be highly effective and efficient:

Step 1: Deconstruct jobs to identify the elemental tasks, both current and future

Step 2: Analyze how best to combine humans and automation

Step 3: Determine the best arrangement to engage talent with the work

Step 4: Reconstruct the work, clearly highlighting the evolving skills profile, including the skills declining in importance, the skills growing in importance, and the skills whose application is changing as AI and automation augment the work[2]

Let's drill into each of these steps to highlight the key questions that must be answered for each.

Step 1: Deconstruct Jobs

Job deconstruction starts by isolating the relevant work elements (such as tasks, activities, or projects) and identifying new elements that are also pertinent. Here, "relevant" means necessary or pivotal to achieving a process outcome, constituent need, or organizational strategic goal. The following questions can help in assessing and understanding work elements:

- What current activities/tasks are still relevant?
- What current activities/tasks are no longer relevant?
- What new relevant activities/tasks must be included?
- What is the timing or sequence of the relevant tasks?
- Where/how/when/what tasks should be performed and by whom?
- What are the skills (technical and enabling) required to perform these tasks?

Step 2: Analyze How Best to Combine Humans and Automation

Combining humans and automation requires an understanding of the work's characteristics, the task's objective, and the automation's role. To achieve this, the following questions should be considered:

- What are the characteristics of each task (repetitive versus variable, mental versus physical, independent versus interactive)?
- What is the objective we are trying to solve for each task? This involves understanding the relationship between the task's performance and the

value delivered to the organization from this performance. We delve
into this issue of return on improved performance (ROIP) below.

- Does automation substitute for the human, augment the human, or create new work?

- What are the available types of automation (robotic process automation, cognitive automation—including machine learning, deep learning, and generative AI—or social or collaborative robotics)?

- What is the optimal way to combine human and automated work across jobs and processes?

A critical step in work design involves understanding how improved performance creates value, a concept referred to as ROIP.[3] While ROIP can take many forms, we can illustrate its significance with four prototypical ROIP relationships. We will use tax preparation as an example here.

- **Eliminate mistakes:** This type of ROIP is most applicable when performance differences range from very low to the minimally acceptable. For tax form preparation, this would range from performance at a very low level, characterized by many mistakes or missed deadlines , to a minimally acceptable performance level that generates a small positive value. For tax preparation, by reducing mistakes, ROIP would entail completing forms correctly and on time.

- **Reduce variance:** This type of ROIP applies when performance differences have no impact on value, as when there are many ways to reach the same goal. Reducing variance produces value not in improving the outcome but rather in reaching that outcome more uniformly, often reducing costs or confusion. For tax preparation, this would include completing the tax form at any time before the due date since getting the tax form completed earlier adds no more value than completing the form on time. Another example is workers assembling components in different sequences, with the final assembly being essentially identical.

- **Incrementally improve value:** This type of ROIP is used when performance improvement produces a constant incremental increase in value. In tax form preparation, this ROIP range might reflect the clarity and grammar quality of the summary letter accompanying a client's tax form. A minimally clear letter satisfies the minimum requirement. Still, a letter that is more clearly written or points out more important highlights is incrementally more valuable to the client and the organization.

Another example is when a call center representative upsells customers by suggesting additional features or faster shipping.

- **Exponentially improve value:** This type of ROIP occurs when improved performance increases value exponentially. This range often represents a rare or creative performance that surprises and delights a customer or disruptively improves a process. In tax form preparation, this ROIP might reflect discovering an obscure tax deduction or a very sophisticated way to restate income to significantly reduce taxes owed. It could also involve an in-store retail associate or call center representative uncovering obscure customer information that reveals a customer's unusual need for higher-margin products or services.

These are the guiding questions for ROIP for each work element:

- Will improved performance eliminate mistakes?
- Will improved performance reduce variance?
- Will improved performance incrementally improve value?
- Will improved performance exponentially improve value?

Let's take the example of robots in hospitals to illustrate the value of the questions above:

1. What are the elemental tasks within the process? Rather than ask, "Will robots replace nurses?" we deconstruct the nursing job and notice that some nursing time is spent checking patients and doing very routine tasks like taking temperatures. In contrast, other time is spent on tasks that more fully use nursing credentials, such as attending to patient crises and administering medication.

2. What are the characteristics of each task (repetitive versus variable, mental versus physical, independent versus interactive)? Now, we can see that the tasks of checking to see if a patient responds to a greeting and taking their temperature are repetitive, physical, and only slightly interactive, making these tasks ripe for automation. On the other hand, tasks such as attending to patient crises and administering medication are more variable, mental, and interactive, making them appropriate for human nurses and more fitting with nurse qualifications.

3. What objective are we trying to solve for each task? Tasks such as taking a temperature and getting a response to a greeting add value mostly by being done to a minimum standard and avoiding obvious mistakes. On

the other hand, tasks such as attending to patient crises and administering medication must meet a very high standard, where the quality of performance greatly affects the outcome. Of course, having nurses take patients' temperatures might help a patient's recovery through the positive effects of human social interactions. This is a good example of how job deconstruction clarifies how the work serves the objective. Separating the tasks of human interaction from taking temperatures allows us to see that if nurses routinely administer medications to patients, human interaction will still occur.

4. Does automation substitute for the human, augment the human, or create new work? Now that we have isolated the deconstructed tasks, we can see that robots can substitute for the human nurse in taking temperatures and checking on patients. In some ways, this automation has augmented the human nurse by freeing them to focus on tasks where their capabilities are far more pivotal.

5. What are the available types of automation (robotic process automation, cognitive automation, or social or collaborative robotics)? Automating the task of taking temperatures and checking on patients might be done with robotic process automation, where a patient monitor might feed the data directly into a database. The solution might also use cognitive automation (or AI) if the patient monitors are programmed to alert nurses when a patient shows a pattern of unresponsiveness or has a series of consecutive high-temperature readings. Finally, the solution might use social robotics, where robots physically move among patients and interact with the nurses.

6. What is the optimal way to combine human and automated work across jobs and processes? By deconstructing the nurse's job, we can now see that a careful combination of a human nurse and a robotic assistant optimizes the work process. This redefines the work beyond the nurse job description. It also means that nurses are now likely to collaborate closely with robotics designers, technicians, and maintenance persons.

Step 2 is increasingly a pivotal one for every organization given the rapid proliferation and adoption of various generative AI tools. Understanding where human activity should be substituted by generative AI, where it should be augmented, and where the presence of generative AI will create the space for new human work or the demand for new human skills will increasingly be a requirement of every leader.

Step 3: Determine the Best Arrangement to Engage Talent with the Work

Once we have determined the optimal combinations of humans and automation, our next step involves determining the best work arrangement to connect talent to work beyond merely defaulting to regular full-time employment in jobs. Optimal solutions seldom directly substitute an alternative work arrangement for an entire job. Rather, the optimum solution is apparent only if we deconstruct the job and examine how each task is best accomplished and the skills required.

Three fundamental dimensions and questions define and suggest how to optimize alternative work arrangements:[4]

1. The assignment (the work to be done)
   a. How small can it be deconstructed?
   b. How widely can it be dispersed?
   c. How far from employment can it be detached?
2. The organization (the boundary containing the work)
   a. How easily can the organization boundary be permeated?
   b. How strongly should the organization link with others?
   c. How deeply should the task involve collaboration?
   d. How extensively should the boundary be flexed to include others?
3. The rewards (the elements of exchange for the work)
   a. How small or immediate is the time frame?
   b. How specifically should they be individualized?
   c. How creatively can we imagine rewards beyond traditional pay and benefits?

For example, organizations have the job of product designer, which includes many tasks. One of those tasks is generating ideas for new products or features, combined with other tasks such as evaluating those ideas to fit with existing production or marketing strategies and selling the ideas to key organization constituents. If we deconstruct the job, the task of generating new product ideas emerges as one "assignment" that can be deconstructed from the rest of the job. Volunteer focus groups can undertake that task, perhaps composed of regular customers, dispersed to a wide array of volunteers, and detached from an employment contract. The "organization" boundary must be permeated only enough to allow the volunteers to interact with product design teams. The rewards consist of free products or just the fun of participating and can be offered immediately.

However, notice that if the question is framed as "Can volunteer focus groups do the job of product designer?" the answer is simply "No," and this alternative does not present itself. Similarly, if the question is framed as "How can we design a job that only suggests new products and features?" the answer is "impossible" because the organization does not have enough of such work to fill a regular job.

Once work is deconstructed, the individual tasks present a much wider range of human work options. The options might include employees in full- or part-time jobs at your location, employees in full- or part-time jobs at other locations, employees in other parts of your organization who you could tap for a project or assignment, independent contractors (either engaged directly or through gig platforms like Upwork and Toptal), the talent of an outsourcer, or the talent of an alliance partner.

Step 4: Reconstruct the Work

Now that activities have been deployed to various alternative means, is there an opportunity for reconstructing new and fundamentally different jobs? This involves answering the following questions:

- How much time has been freed up?
- What skills are no longer required as a result, and what skills remain important?
- What new work might be combined with the work that remains?
- What are the adjacent skills to those that remain?

As you can see, work design is critical to moving beyond the one-to-one relationship between jobholders and jobs and the high frictional cost of such limiting arrangements to the many-to-many relationships between skills and work required to power the agile, twenty-first-century enterprise. Now that we have explored the core process of work design, let's discuss the new rules of leadership that are required to execute this process:

1. From narrow definitions of cost and performance to all-encompassing metrics: Many organizations manage the component costs of work individually. We are all too familiar with reductions in force that are pursued to reduce headcount, only to find that the work remains and contractor

expenses have now spiked. In *Work without Jobs*, the authors introduced the idea of the total cost of work (TCoW).[5] TCoW is defined as total labor cost (e.g., full-time employees, free agents, gig workers) plus vendor cost (e.g., outsourcing cost, AI, and robotics vendor cost) plus annualized capital charge for relevant capitalized investments (e.g., company-developed AI or robotics, equity stakes in third-party work options). It is important to compare all work options on a uniform basis to ensure the analysis is not distorted by variations in accounting treatment (e.g., labor cost is expensed, while the investment in robotics is capitalized). One should multiply the company's cost of capital by the total capital investment in work options like AI/robotics and alliances to capture the annualized charge for using these options.

2. From defining management as delegation, supervision, and coordination to a broader concept of orchestration: Leaders of traditional job-based organizations rely on traditional hierarchies and focus their resource management efforts on delegating authority, supervising the talent performing the work, and coordinating disparate activities across processes to achieve specific outcomes. To redesign work to optimize the various options discussed, orchestration is important. This requires not only real insight into each option, including their cost, value, and risks, but also knowing when to choose one option over another option, and how to synergize the output from gig workers with machine learning insights to enable an employee to deliver a new product. Orchestration is a critical enabler of work design.

3. From siloed to boundaryless work: Realizing the full potential of work design requires thinking beyond traditional functional, geographic, and other organizational boundaries. For example, how often have you heard something like, "Robotic process automation would be ideal for this body of work, but we would need to engage a vendor and go through the whole IT and procurement process," only to discover later that your finance function already has a vendor in place, excess server capacity, and an underused bot library, making your cost of using robotic process automation negligible?

Let's shift our attention to the technology-enabling work design as a capability. We are seeing an increasing number of AI-driven tools emerge to help organizations build this capability of work design. One example is

Mercer's work design tool, which equips leaders to redesign work at speed and scale. This tool deconstructs jobs into tasks, recommends redeployment options (e.g., robotic process automation, machine learning, gig talent, shared services) based on the tasks' characteristics and profile, and supports the reconstruction of new work based on an analysis of skill adjacencies, all while shining a spotlight on the shifting skills profile (i.e., the ones increasing versus decreasing in importance as work is redesigned). Figure 4.2 depicts screenshots from the tool and the analysis of the shifting skills profile for a certified medical assistant whose job is being redesigned.

Talent Deployment

As you saw with work design, and as we have previously discussed with the fixed, flex, and flow models, one of the key benefits of the skills-powered organization is the deeper insight into the demand and supply of skills and the opportunity to redeploy talent based on the matching of skills to work at a scale and speed previously not possible with the traditional job-based model. As was the case for work design, this capability of talent deployment is underpinned by the same three critical enablers:

1. Process: Traditional talent deployment processes are based on the stable movement of talent from one job to another (the fixed model). As described in chapter 2, a skills-powered organization affords us the flexibility to consider other means—flexible and flow models—for deploying talent to work. Leveraging a common skills taxonomy, these two models are predicated on having a process and technology platform for an internal talent marketplace that enables skills to be the currency of work and talent deployment. The key steps underpinning the process are the following:

   a. Insight into what skills are demanded: Managers, supported by the AI that powers talent marketplaces, define the skills underlying the tasks that need to be performed. As we described in the work design capability, there are new tools that allow this to be done more seamlessly.

   b. Insight into the supply of skills both within and outside the organization: Virtually all the talent marketplace technologies provide some level of skills inference. As illustrated in the introduction, companies like SkyHive have advanced this capability to an art form.

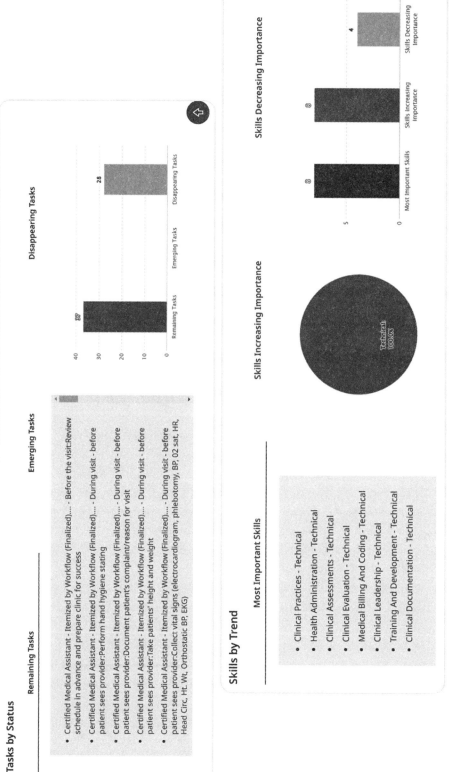

Figure 4.2

Analysis of evolving tasks and the skill implications as work is redesigned

c. Matching of demand and supply: While these technologies' algorithms can clearly show where someone might be a good fit for a project or assignment, executing the process requires more than just presenting someone with a list of projects they are eligible for. It often requires nudges and incentives. For example, at Google, workers are free to apply for any role, but recommended icons for certain roles indicate company-preferred matches, helping them narrow down the opportunities presented. Other companies use incentives to encourage employees to choose specific high-priority assignments.

2. New rules for leadership

   a. From "owned" talent to talent as an enterprise asset: This challenge has been a bugbear for HR leaders since the beginning, but addressing it is pivotal to making a skills-powered organization work. It requires leaders to move beyond their traditional parochial view of talent, often reinforced by their budgets.

   b. From managing budgets to "giving and getting" capability: Achieving this shift often requires creative solutions. For example, some organizations have mandated that 5 to 15 percent of all new work be posted on the talent marketplace before a leader is allowed to open a new hire requisition.

   c. From hierarchical authority to empowering and enabling: Our traditional model of leadership reinforces the notion of hierarchical authority, but leading talent who are connecting to your work through short-term projects, assignments, and gigs requires a different mindset as talent now has the choice of whether to engage with your work or not. Leaders with a brand for empowering and enabling talent to contribute, develop, and grow will have a significant advantage over their less-evolved peers.

3. Technology: In chapter 5 we will be exploring in detail the technology— and the pivotal role of AI—that enables insight into skills demand and supply, the matching of skills to work, the matching of developmental resources to close skills gaps, and the management of data and insight to ensure the continuous and seamless link between work, talent, and learning.

Unilever has long been regarded as a leader in using a skills-powered talent marketplace to deploy talent. In 2020, the company rolled out Unilever

Flex—inviting its workforce to "live your purpose," "upskill," and "do something exciting and different from your daily job." The following are some of the results the company realized:

700+ projects resourced in 90 days

60 percent of projects resourced cross-functionally and cross-geographically

4,200+ projects posted by businesses across the globe

27,000 Unilever employees using Flex

530,000 unlocked hours—equivalent to the workload of 241 full-time employees

90 percent of employees learned something new and would do it again

82 percent of project owners were highly satisfied with talent from Flex[6]

Talent Development

As we discussed in the introduction to this book, one of the great benefits of the skills-powered organization is its ability to ensure seamless and timely matching of the demand for work with the supply of skills while shining a spotlight on any gaps and mismatches and correcting these by directing the appropriate learning and developmental resources to talent. This "holy grail" of organizational development ensures that the pivotal role of development in executing the business model is explicitly accounted for. Organizations that prioritize development and make it the cornerstone of their talent value propositions will increasingly be the winners in the war for talent. Let's explore our three key enablers for making talent development a core capability:

1. Process: The traditional talent development process prioritizes employment qualifications over work readiness. Employment qualifications are typically limited to the headline technical skills required to perform a job. However, as value shifts from technical to enabling skills, development must retool accordingly. Talent can increasingly acquire technical skills quickly and cheaply through the numerous nano- and micro-upskilling opportunities available through various online learning resources. These resources also give talent a clear understanding of adjacencies. For example, graphic design and 3D animation are adjacent skills because the work of graphic design can be upskilled to 3D

animation work. On the other hand, although they share some common attributes, Python programming is not closely related to graphic design. It takes many more hours and a longer pathway to go from Python to 3D animation even though 3D animation may be done on software that uses Python programming. As technical skills become increasingly easy to acquire and change, development will need to focus on enabling skills. The taxonomies that underpin talent marketplaces allow organizations to elevate these enabling skills and afford them the visibility and developmental resources required.

2. New rules for leadership: Given the shrinking half-life of many technical skills, the quantum and velocity of development are increasing exponentially. Leaders will need to transform their legacy view of development as a discretionary expense that is typically at the top of the list when budget reductions are called for to viewing it as a mission-critical investment, pivotal to executing their strategies. The direct connections between the demand for work and the link to development resources to close the underlying skill gaps should help them make this shift. A leader will need to explicitly design space for learning in the flow of work as the volume and speed of upskilling and reskilling no longer make it feasible for talent to "do it on their own time."

3. Technology: As mentioned above, the technology and underlying AI are pivotal to providing insight into the appropriate development resource and access. Again, we will explore this technology dimension in much greater detail in chapter 5.

Now that we have explored our three core capabilities for driving the skills-powered organization, let's explore how Standard Chartered is building its talent development and deployment capabilities by moving away from traditional frameworks that relied on past performance and experience as being predictors of future potential, to focusing on the actual skills required and the aspirations to develop them.

Making Skills the Currency of Talent Development and Deployment Processes at Standard Chartered

As part of Standard Chartered's focus on strengthening the way it developed and deployed skills, it recently refreshed its approach to identifying the potential of its workforce and connecting them to the evolving demand for work. To deliver on its strategic aspirations, it was important to identify talent who could demonstrate the skills and aspiration to perform the critical work of the future while ensuring those skills were available at the right time and accessible to the right teams. The new approach thus moved away from the traditional emphasis on past performance and experiences as the primary predictors of potential and future capability to instead focus on an individual's ability against a defined set of skills coupled with their underlying aspirations.

Skills provide insight into an individual's ability to take on more complex work in the future, while aspirations indicate if the right interest, drive, and energy are all present to effectively apply the skills. So, to holistically assess an individual's ability to contribute in the future, an individual's aspiration to progress in their career has to be accompanied by proficiency in key skills and a desire to put those skills into action through ever more complex responsibilities. Pivoting to this approach has been critical to enabling the shift toward making skills the new currency of work across the organization.

Based on research conducted by various external partners on the profiles of thousands of individuals across various industries, as well as predictive analysis of the link between different skills and multiple success metrics, specific skills were identified that were fit for purpose for its unique context and specific performance requirements. Strongly linked to the leadership agreement (which we explored in chapter 1) and the valued behaviors, these skills are the ability to grow, collaborate, execute, and lead. Underpinning these skills is the core enabling skill of learning agility; the ability to learn from successes, failures, experimentation, and feedback while applying learning to new problems and opportunities; and working through ambiguity and change while being adaptable. These skills are increasingly underpinning hiring, promotion, and development decisions.

The underlying philosophy of this approach is that all employees have the potential to contribute to the evolving needs of the business. To meet their fullest potential and stretch further, they need to be engaged, motivated, and developed to enable them to deliver in their current role and the firm's future needs. Delivering on these future needs and performance ambitions requires talent to be developed and deployed to the areas of greatest opportunity. This begins with identifying colleagues with the greatest potential to contribute: those who exhibit high levels of ambition, consistently demonstrate key skills through action, and have the learning agility to take on bigger challenges. The goal is to further accelerate these employees' development speed and take targeted action to enhance their impact.

People leaders play a critical role in this approach of development and deployment. Potential needs to be understood in the context of current and future aspirations—providing insight into the willingness of employees to apply their skills. It is not assessed solely by people leaders but is part of a two-way dialogue between the individual and their leaders. People leaders are expected to engage in regular, quality conversations with their teams to understand their aspirations and assess their proficiency against the key skills to determine their future potential. Detailed guidance is provided to leaders on the specific indicators associated with each skill and the expectations at different levels of the organization. Leaders are provided with the probing questions they should be asking to understand their team members' interests, aspirations, and readiness for acquiring new skills and taking on challenges to determine their level of ambition to take on more accountability and to apply their skills to drive greater impact.

Guidance is also provided to people leaders on how they can support their teams in developing their skills by leveraging resources and opportunities to curate and personalize learning experiences. They are also educated on how to take targeted action to deploy the skills of the talent ready for a bigger challenge. Moreover, they are taught that future potential is not fixed and can develop and change over time. This perspective is encouraged by them having the flexibility to update their team's potential assessment in the talent management system at any time throughout the year. While all colleagues are prepopulated in the system as talent who should be stretched to reinforce the importance of unlocking potential, people leaders are encouraged to conduct regular reviews of their talent and tag whom they believe are ready to be accelerated into new opportunities. Going forward, the aspiration is to be able to leverage the people leaders' assessment to populate skills passports, which can provide a reliable, enterprise view of employees' skills to be able to use this information to deploy these skills to different parts of the enterprise, agnostic of "job" or function. This will create informed talent deployment decisions and more optimal talent matching to work as it is redesigned to incorporate evolving business needs and emerging automation.

The net impact of this approach to assessing skills and aspiration is the execution of a talent strategy that provides bespoke developmental interventions and targeted career opportunities for the highest potential talent, enabling them to deploy their skills more rapidly in roles and assignments that are increasingly pivotal to executing the business strategy. That same talent strategy ensures a consistent proposition to the entire workforce: continuous growth, skill development, and access to opportunity. It is predicated on individual accountability and is supported by an evolving technology architecture to enable continuous skill building.

The HR team further expects to leverage insights from this assessment process to feed into its strategic workforce planning process. For example, if a low percentage of the organization's workforce is identified as "accelerate," that could indicate a weak internal talent pipeline and a lack of skills required to execute the business strategy. This could lead to a greater reliance on external hiring for the needed skills. Conversely, a higher percentage of talent categorized as accelerate could indicate a need to review the assessment process to ensure that employee expectations are balanced with the available opportunities. This is essential to minimizing disappointment in a perceived inability to progress and any potential knock-on consequences to employee engagement and attrition of valuable talent.

5 The Role of AI in Building a Skills-Powered Organization

As we are seeing, AI is pivotal to powering the skills-powered organization. Before we get any deeper into how AI is being applied, let's start with a quick summary of what it is and how it has evolved.

To date, we have had four generations of AI:

- **First generation:** Rule-based systems. Also known as expert systems, these systems are the earliest form of AI, and they operate based on a predefined set of rules and logic programmed by human experts. An example of such a system would be applicant tracking systems (ATS). Used in recruitment and hiring, these systems automatically screen resumes and applications based on predefined criteria such as keywords, skills, experience, and education. For example, if a job requires a specific skill certification, an ATS can be programmed to reject applications that do not mention this certification.

- **Second generation:** Machine learning. This type of AI can learn and improve from experience without being explicitly programmed. Unlike rule-based systems, machine learning algorithms use statistical methods to find patterns in massive amounts of data. They learn from this data and make predictions or decisions based on it rather than following predefined rules. An example of machine learning is personalized learning and development programs for employees. By analyzing an employee's job role, skills, performance, and career goals, machine learning algorithms can recommend the most relevant and effective learning programs for each individual to close skills gaps or to prepare someone for a role they aspire to.

- **Third generation:** Deep learning. This subset of machine learning uses neural networks with multiple layers; hence the term "deep." Deep learning models are designed to learn from experience automatically and adaptively by using complex structures, known as artificial neural networks, inspired by the human brain. An example of deep learning would be resume screening, where deep learning algorithms can screen resumes and rank candidates based on their suitability for a job. Unlike traditional keyword-based screening, deep learning can understand the context and nuances of the information in a resume, making the screening process more accurate and efficient.

- **Fourth generation:** Generative AI. This type of AI focuses on generating new content that resembles the data on which it was trained. This can include various outputs, such as text, images, music, and even voice. The key aspect of generative AI is that the output is new and original, not just a repetition of the input data. Consider our personalized learning example using machine learning. Instead of the limited permutations possible with machine learning, generative AI can analyze an employee's skills, performance, and career goals to generate personalized career development plans or suggest suitable jobs, gigs, or learning opportunities. Generative AI can act as a personal coach to an employee, continuously inferring skills as they are developed and recommending learning and other resources to guide career development.

In a stable world where jobs are the singular currency of work, AI may seem like a luxury. Still, the quantum pace of changing skills demand, the many-to-many relationships between skills and work, and the need to upskill and reskill at pace and scale make AI a necessity. The algorithms that underpin talent platforms like Eightfold, SkyHive, TechWolf, and Gloat, to name a few of the dozens of skills-related technologies out there, are pivotal for helping leaders understand

- the demand for skills;
- the supply of skills (internally and/or externally);
- the matching of skills to work through gigs, projects, jobs, and assignments; and
- the matching of learning and developmental resources for closing skills gaps.

Let's explore these areas in turn and illustrate how AI addresses each challenge before we delve into how Standard Chartered is it to transform its business.

The Demand for Skills

Recall our insurance company example from chapter 2 and how the movement from the fixed to the flow model enabled much earlier and stronger signals of changing skills demand, as all data science work was being performed using the marketplace, and the AI continually assesses how the demand for skills is changing as various projects are posted to the marketplace. Deep learning algorithms like this can help organizations identify the skills required by various bodies of work. For example, TechWolf can infer skills from Jira and Asana projects. Similarly, Eightfold can identify skills within a job description, find candidates, and then identify trending and adjacent skills through its sophisticated models. In addition, platforms like the Mercer work design tool described in chapter 4 can provide a snapshot of how work can be redesigned as well as the changing skills required as tasks are redeployed to alternative work options or augmented by AI and automation.

The Supply of Skills

By analyzing data from thousands of different sources and generating their own proprietary data, platforms like SkyHive and Eightfold have the functionality to provide visibility into real-time labor market movements at a skill level. While knowing the supply of skills externally is useful, understanding the skills of your current talent is essential to driving the skills-powered organization. Recall the example in the introduction of how SkyHive's AI could infer people's skills from their current and previous roles, experiences, and education. Similarly, the Eightfold platform collects, indexes, and analyzes millions and millions of talent profiles and uses AI to match them to jobs, opportunities, and career paths. It also looks at adjacent skills; professional contacts; companies you have worked for; and the time spent in various jobs, education, and work locations—all of which help provide a more comprehensive view of an individual's skills. For example, if you worked at Microsoft in 2023, you probably learned about Open AI's generative AI technology. Still, if you worked at Salesforce two years prior, you know all about a different technology stack. Like SkyHive, Eightfold's algorithm aims to infer skills from jobs and a much broader data set. While companies have traditionally relied on skill and other assessments to understand their talent supply, AI-driven skills inferencing adds a powerful new dimension. While traditional skill assessments show potential capability, skill inferencing shows demonstrated capability and possible adjacencies.

The Matching of Skills to Work through Gigs, Projects, Jobs, and Assignments

The matching of skills to work is the very essence of what a talent marketplace does. External marketplaces like Upwork, Fiverr, and Topcoder have matched gig talent to work for years. Internal talent marketplaces like Gloat and Fuel50 can infer talent skills within organizations and match them to career opportunities, jobs, gigs, projects, and assignments. The deep learning algorithms of these platforms match information on the skills demanded for various types of work to the skills supplied by talent across the organization, including adjacent skills, enabling the continuous matching of talent to work as demand and supply evolve.

Learning and Developmental Resources to Close Skills Gaps

The final area in using AI to drive the skills-powered organization is deploying developmental resources to close identified skill gaps. AI can analyze an individual's current skill set and recommend learning and other resources to help them acquire the skills required for various jobs, projects, assignments, and gigs. This can help talent identify the skills they must develop to qualify for a particular role or project and ensure that they stay up-to-date with the latest industry trends and evolving demand for skills by accessing learning resources, training, certifications, mentoring, and other developmental resources. This is an area that generative AI is transforming. It can do the following:

- Generate personalized development plans for employees based on their performance and strengths/weaknesses.
- Create engaging and interactive learning activities like games and simulations to help employees understand complex concepts and reskill at speed.

- Generate real-time feedback and assessments, allowing the learning function and leaders to quickly identify areas where employees need additional support to close skills gaps.
- Create customized learning content (e.g., text, images, audio, video) at speed and scale to enable large-scale talent transitions as companies restructure, enabling talent redeployment at scale and speed.

New Skills for a New Way of Working as Every Employee Needs AI Aptitude

As AI (particularly generative AI) permeates every facet of our lives and becomes an increasingly critical tool for business, it is both helping us to better analyze and manage skills as we have illustrated and changing the very skills required of each of us to operate in this AI-augmented world. According to the 2023 Microsoft Work Trend Index, analytical judgment (understanding where AI should substitute versus augment human capability), flexibility (the ability to adjust rapidly to AI's integration in the workflow), and emotional intelligence (determining when to leverage a human capability instead of AI) were among the top of the list of skills leaders believed will be essential for employees in an AI-powered future.[1] Other critical skills included creative evaluation (the ability to evaluate the content produced by AI), intellectual curiosity (asking AI the right questions), bias detection (evaluating AI fairness in decision-making), and AI delegation (directing AI with the right prompts).

More recently, Microsoft Viva has made significant advances in accomplishing all four of these objectives within a single platform. The Skills in Viva system is not just an engine for inference the supply of skills but also a skills-powered learning system, an employee development platform, and an internal mobility tool that looks like a talent marketplace.[2] It has the potential to be incredibly disruptive to the marketplace of skills-focused technologies given Microsoft's installed base of corporate users. The skills engine in Viva is built on the taxonomy of skills from LinkedIn's Skills Graph and infers skills from all employee activity in Microsoft Graph. As Skills in Viva expands in usage, it will bring in skills from various external systems and give employees many ways to curate, view, and update their skills.

Now that we have explored why AI is so critical to driving the skills-powered organization, let's explore Standard Chartered's journey and application of it.

AI at Standard Chartered

To say that the internal talent marketplace at Standard Chartered has been only about enabling a stronger development and growth culture would be too simplistic a view. While that was a part of the consideration (as you read in chapter 3), there was deep commerciality embedded in the decision to introduce this piece of technology.

As the firm started to invest in building future-ready skills across its workforce, the leadership team was acutely conscious of the need to be able to deploy these skills in an accelerated manner to the areas of biggest opportunity so they could deliver impact for clients and a better return for shareholders. The COVID-19 pandemic further underscored the need for redeploying skills at scale and speed. Identifying the skills that are in supply (within the existing workforce) and the skills that are needed, especially to stay relevant in the future of banking—across an organization of over eighty-five thousand employees in over fifty markets—is a task (and experience) that only technology can enable, with data, analytics, and AI doing the heavy lifting. The enormity of it all begins to become apparent when it is acknowledged that the skills that employees possess are an amalgamation of the experiences they have had across all of their jobs and projects, not just the degrees they have earned or the learning programs they have attended. And adding to the complexity is that these skills continuously evolve.

But even before the challenge of matching thousands of skills to hundreds of projects (or gigs, as work is currently represented in constructs beyond jobs), the earliest hurdle that would be faced in the skills journey was the absence of a universal language for talking about skills. While it already had robust competency frameworks in place, these have been aligned to the jobs that people do and hence could only partially cover the skills they possess or the skills of the future that the firm needs. Machine learning algorithms that can cleanse, understand, and relate skills data without needing the company to undertake the creation of a bespoke skills taxonomy became critical to experimenting with skills-powered deployment—a key capability of an internal talent marketplace platform.

The underlying algorithm of the internal marketplace platform intelligently matches people with a range of opportunities based on their skills, experiences, interests, and aspirations. It gives full visibility to skills and experiences across markets, making it easier to find, develop, and deploy the right people to the right challenges to solve. The AI can continuously rematch and realign talent to relevant areas of need and focus, meeting changing demands as the organization evolves in response to a dynamic operating environment. And a consumer-grade UX enables employees to have a direct dialogue with other colleagues, make connections, and collaborate outside traditional silos, unlocking massive potential with minimal friction.

For example, when the entity in India wanted to define a blueprint for rolling out "deaf-friendly banking" across markets, and build a scalable framework that could create an ecosystem for delivering an exceptional client experience through the sign language servicing channel, the core team knew that they needed a range of skills to accomplish this, not all of which they possessed. These included tech skills to review the existing video banking tool and the client experience to identify improvements needed; risk analysis and risk management skills to identify, evaluate, and report on the risks in the proposed solution to aid remediation; project management skills for driving streamlined end-to-end design and delivery; and branding and marketing skills to build a go-to-market strategy for the proof-of-concept solution.

Instead of asking for additional headcount and budgets (a time-consuming exercise in any firm), the core team used the internal talent marketplace to crowdsource the skills needed for delivering this program in an ambitious timeframe. A colleague with a communications background who was also leading a local diversity and inclusion employee resource group was matched to the gig as were a user acceptance testing manager who brought skills in cloud computing and quality assurance, a colleague from the tax team who had prior audit and process documentation experience, and a tech product head who had program management skills. All of them were located in different offices across India. Within four months, not only was a scalable framework ready to launch the sign language servicing to all clients in India, but the team had also begun sharing implementation opportunities with other markets. Aptly, this gig had been titled "Breaking the Silence" on the marketplace.

The marketplace has helped organically identify that, based on user profiles, some of the top skills in supply internally are project management, risk management, business requirements analysis, financial analysis and reporting, and key performance indicator design. At the same time, when looking at the opportunities posted on the platform, the top skills in demand were communication, project planning and management, risk management, Microsoft Excel, data analysis, and analytical skills. It also helped determine that general management, risk management, finance, and leadership skills were the top skills employees aspired to develop.

As the AI in the marketplace is connecting this skills supply and aspiration data with the skills demand data, and talent is being deployed to gigs, the organization can unlock capacity and increase productivity. What started as the unlocking of 14,000 hours of productivity, equivalent to $584,000, via less than 300 gigs during the pilot in India in 2020 has now resulted in productivity worth $6 million that has been realized over the course of 1,700+ gigs since the pilot was first initiated. Not surprisingly, many of the gigs on the marketplace have been linked to sustainability and digital innovation, underscoring the increasing ability to direct employees' energies toward areas of strategic importance for the firm and help employees build skills around these future-focused topics.

Focused change enablement efforts have been critical to scaling the adoption of the internal talent marketplace among employees to sign up and among people leaders to post gigs. It has required an entire ecosystem to be established such that deployment efforts balance a global framework with local need. While business leaders as sponsors continue to be important for messaging top-down, it is the network of change champions established as the scale-up happens who have often been at the heart of driving the narrative. These change champions bring on-the-ground insights to support the launch in their market/business/function as well as share active feedback and cocreate with the HR teams. They help drive understanding of the platform among their peers, encouraging them to sign up on the talent marketplace and sourcing success stories from their network. Even after the initial energy of the launch subsides, they continue to be key advocates for the platform, often having been the first adopters of it.

Similarly, actively capturing employee feedback has been important for driving continuous improvement and evolution of the internal talent marketplace. The HR team regularly conducts drop-in "clinics" to engage with users and gather their feedback. Some of the feedback is also published in the form of success stories. Showcasing these real-life stories has helped generate momentum and build confidence in the value of the skills-powered solution that the platform provides for both building capability and unlocking capacity. Triaging inputs from across sponsors, champions, and employees has helped the internal talent marketplace also undergo a range of enhancements since the initial pilot, including the launch of new features to ensure relevance. While it had started out just as a tool for gigs, the platform now supports mentoring, short-term assignments, permanent positions (all through AI-enabled matching of skills to work), and the new features as part of the work underway in the wholesale banking business (detailed below).

With over twenty-eight thousand employees currently signed up to the internal talent marketplace, the platform has the potential to serve as a critical foundation for Standard Chartered's transformation to being a skills-powered organization. By integrating data from the marketplace with data from other systems, such as its learning platform diSCover, there is opportunity to gain better visibility of its skills landscape, including gaps and learning interventions required, not only to continue building a future-ready workforce but also to better inform strategic workforce planning and critical talent decision-making. There is the potential to make connections between the top skills in demand on the marketplace (as well as the skills that employees aspire to build) with some of the developmental programs (future skills academies) that have been rolled out—such as Data and Analytics Academy and Leadership Academy—to both validate past planning decisions and help inform future agendas. So, while the journey started with an SWP based on the "traditional" concept of jobs (as shared in chapter 2), the organization is now leveraging the last three years' experience to make further inroads toward making both work and the employee experience increasingly skills powered.

The corporate and investment banking business—which provides financing, investment, treasury, and strategic advisory services (typically called wholesale banking in the sector)—is leading the way in this. This business, one of the three global divisions, supports over twenty thousand clients in the world's fastest-growing economies by facilitating global trade, capital, and investment flows. It is taking the initial learnings on skills development and deployment to make further, firmer advancements into becoming more skills powered. Business leaders have partnered closely with HR colleagues to build skills-powered, future-focused profiles for around thirty job families (such as sustainable finance bankers and quants), which are critical for delivering the business strategy and meeting client needs.

Additionally, the business is enabling integration across technology platforms to allow individual employees and people leaders to assess skill levels, including benchmarking with the market. It uses the information to suggest specific skill-building avenues for developmental areas (both content-based learning and on-the-job experiences) and suggest skill deployment and career opportunities based on areas of strength and skills adjacency. All of this is being enabled through AI on the internal talent marketplace, delivering hyperpersonalized input for employees to guide their development and career journeys, enabling them to transcend traditional linear development pathways in literally one click.

Imagine this scenario: a corporate banking RM might be recommended three career paths based on their skills and aspirations. They could then be offered nine different gigs or projects, along with eighteen different learning modules to upskill in areas needed to progress on these paths. Now imagine this happening tens of thousands of times—with thousands of many-to-many connections happening as skills are matched to evolving work. The aggregate workforce intelligence gathered through this marketplace then better informs the business in making strategic resourcing decisions on the skills it needs to "buy" versus "build" versus "borrow."

As this work lands and eventually scales, the leadership and HR teams are expecting that an even more integrated, seamless experience will continue to drive greater adoption of the marketplace, increasing the network effect whereby increasing numbers of users—both people posting high-quality gigs and those looking for gigs—will enhance the ability of the marketplace to serve its purpose of connecting skills with work and building future-focused skills. The ambition is for these tools to be increasingly embedded in the flow of work. Today, the marketplace is already helping accelerate agile ways of working by helping multidisciplinary teams to quickly connect and execute on priorities. Additionally, when hiring, managers and internal recruiters are often evaluating business needs for potential new roles or replacement role holders. When the conversation steers toward a solution to manage the interim state while a hire is being identified and onboarded, there is an opportunity for putting different tasks that comprise the role into the marketplace—the temporary deconstruction of a job—and tapping into talent in different parts of the organization to help deliver the work.

The leadership team has long considered technology to be key to providing and scaling tailored experiences (both for employees and clients) as well as for driving the skills-powered workforce agenda that is critical for staying relevant in the fast-evolving world of financial services. However, they also acknowledge that technology is, to an extent, only an enabler. The marketplace is nudging employees to change how they think about work, deliver outcomes, and collaborate with each other in the process, emulating the expectations that employees have of the workplace: flexibility, choice, and transparency. While we spoke in chapter 3 about employees having to acclimatize to the massive shift in how they learn, there's an even greater shift in the expectations from people leaders and how they lead in an environment where team boundaries are blurring. Leaders need to get even more comfortable with talent sharing as their team members develop and deploy their skills in completely different parts of the firm. As we describe in chapter 4, leaders need to stretch their thinking beyond the notion of a job being the currency of work. They also need to able to deconstruct it into tasks and identify the underlying skills needed to deliver these tasks, while determining the various options for executing these tasks (e.g., crowdsourcing, gig talent), thereby making skills the currency of work.

Finally, the company is also mindful of the risks associated with technology, and especially AI, if it is not designed or delivered using a responsible and ethical framework. Strong governance mechanisms have been established as it continues experimenting with state-of-the-art technologies to create an exceptional employee experience, support informed decision-making, and drive greater operational efficiency.

Deploying an AI solution requires data to identify and formulate the rules, more data to train the system, and yet more data to validate and test it. Also, in addition to large data sets, high-quality data input is required to have a high-quality output. Therefore, from the start, the focus has been on the suitability of the data used in its AI use cases to ensure it is representative of the intended usage and reliable for training the model. This has often required the organization to partner with specialist vendors rather than to develop tools internally. A data set's size and quality become important factors for consideration before selecting a particular vendor—the vendor must have clear guidelines informed by the data scientists who have developed, and continue to evolve, the platform. The developers need to have balanced the data used for training AI models to ensure they meet expected diversity standards and that all demographic groups are fairly represented. By its nature, AI is data hungry, and the more balanced data that the technology has, can account for, and learn from, the better it can control for potential unjust or societal bias.

The use of responsible AI standards is combined with a rigorous human-centered approach to the design and deployment of such tools. To do this in a consistent manner, multiple cross-functional groups have been established—such as the Council for the Responsible Use of AI/ML, the Responsible AI Review Forum, the Fairness (of AI models) Working Group, and the Data Ethics Working Group. These forums and working groups bring together specialists from across technology, data, business, compliance, risk governance, and HR teams who review, challenge, and debate the production, deployment, or implementation of use cases that leverage AI/machine learning techniques before any decisions are taken to move forward with these tools and platforms.

6 The HR Function and Its Role in Orchestrating the Skills-Powered Organization

As the very essence of how talent is connected to work changes and evolves beyond the singular means of connecting jobs and jobholders to the plurality of means that comes from making skills the currency of work, every aspect of how talent is acquired, developed, deployed, rewarded, and engaged needs to change. This chapter will explore the changing role and capabilities of the HR function and its pivot from its traditional role of being a steward of employment to being a steward of work, enabling and advising leaders on how they can address the two pivotal questions we explored in chapter 3. The increased potential and power of AI and automation will also fundamentally transform the function's traditional role from service delivery to work leadership.

While the concept of being skills powered is not brand new, the idea of integrating it across the employee life cycle and the organization's operating model is one that leaders are struggling with. Today, many organizations say there is a "war for talent," but they are fighting a war for the "hot skills" that will disproportionately impact business growth and customer outcomes. The HR function has to play a leadership role in the kind of choices that organizations need to start making to attract and build these hot skills after having helped the business understand the specific skills that underpin the emerging work of the enterprise, how to pivot talent practices around skills, how to make more decisions based on skills, and how to design operating models and (re)design work so that skills can be fluidly developed and deployed to keep pace with work as it evolves. All of this demands a shift in infrastructure, culture, and technology.

To facilitate this shift, four key factors underpin the evolution of the HR function in this new world of work:

1. Its evolving role in driving the skills-powered organization
2. Its "products" for transforming the enterprise architecture from one organized around jobs to skills
3. How it enables and shapes the experience of every person engaging with the organization's work
4. Being obsessively data driven

Let's explore each of these in turn.

The Evolving Role of HR

In its insightful study, "HR4.0: Shaping People Strategies in the Fourth Industrial Revolution," the World Economic Forum explored the shift of the HR function from one primarily focused on service delivery and administration to one that

- determines business outcomes through innovation, creativity, stability, and agility of talent;
- drives the connection between the company and the community;
- influences positive societal outcomes in an era of transformation and disruption;
- is a coarchitect of the organizational culture; and
- is at the forefront of deploying technology in the pursuit of inclusion and efficiency.[1]

The report noted that HR leaders will increasingly need to develop skills related to data analytics, understanding and helping others understand technology; systems thinking; design thinking; storytelling; understanding the emerging field of mapping jobs, skills, and tasks; and conducting strategic workforce planning. While organizations are shifting their business models and transforming work and the workforce, HR professionals often find themselves caught between fulfilling their legacy role and playing the leadership role required in the future. The six key imperatives that HR will need to lead on include the following:

1. Developing new leadership capabilities for the Fourth Industrial Revolution: As organizations operate more distributed business models, leaders will need to lead from the edge, adopt the right technologies, drive a

new vision of organizational culture, and shape innovative people strategies for the future of work.

2. Managing the integration of technology in the workplace: The way work gets done is changing. A growing area of responsibility for HR is to partner with CEOs and C-suite leaders to achieve the optimal combination of human workforce and automation to ensure a positive impact on the future of work.

3. Enhancing the work experience: As we have already explored and will discuss further, the increasing complexity of the workforce and the use of technology are calling for a change in how work is experienced. HR is vital in defining, measuring, and enabling the meaningful employee experience in the Fourth Industrial Revolution.

4. Building an agile and personalized learning culture: HR plays a leading role in fostering a culture of lifelong learning in the context of declining demand for certain skills, the emergence of new ones, and the requirement for talent to continuously learn, unlearn, and relearn.

5. Establishing metrics and analytics for valuing human capital: The mutually beneficial relationship between the workforce, organizations, and society makes it essential for HR to create a compelling case for establishing viable and scalable measures of human capital as a key performance driver and continuously demonstrate the impact of its work on business performance. We will soon explore HR's role in analytics more depth.

6. Embedding diversity and inclusion: Changing social, economic, and political forces allow organizations to profoundly advance inclusion and diversity. HR plays a pivotal role in promoting a sense of purpose and belonging in the workforce and equality and prosperity for the communities and regions in which they operate.

The HR function is transforming faster than it ever has. Progressive CHROs have transformed the very essence of their function, their work, and how its many stakeholders perceive it as they evolve from being a steward of employment to being a steward of work.

HR Products for Evolving the Organization

HR professionals need to increasingly recognize their role as product managers—they are in the business of selling and managing the "work" product—which is at the nexus of talent expectation and business need. While the world is becoming increasingly commoditized, gone are the days of legacy HR one-size-fits-all programs and processes. When one is not competing on experience as a product owner, it's a race to the bottom— similarly, empowerment, and personalization have also become crucial to employees (just as it always has been for consumers). The days of being pre- scriptive in telling people what and how they should learn, collaborate, and deliver work are fading away. Poor product design, technology driven or otherwise, that does not enable choice and flexibility significantly impacts the work experience and the "return on work."

Many in today's workforce are of the generation that experiences better technology and services in their personal lives than they do at work. The HR function needs to identify, understand, and be comfortable with the opportunities to leverage state-of-the-art technologies to make jobs more meaningful, careers more enriching, learning more customized, and work more fun and easier to get done. And all this needs to be enabled at scale.

Like the "hooks" that product managers create to embed their product in consumers' day-to-day habits (or create habits around products), HR profes- sionals must be strong change managers. For example, they must be able to create the pull to drive adoption of new, and at times novel to employees, technology platforms like the internal talent marketplace so that employees do the work of setting up their profiles to allow the algorithm to generate recommendations for projects, potential mentors, or learning opportuni- ties they may never have considered. Or they need to help managers build the habit of turning to such a marketplace to crowdsource skills versus defaulting to opening a new requisition for additional full-time employees. They may also need to build and maintain strong senior sponsorship so that business leaders are encouraging their teams on an ongoing basis to leverage opportunities for skill building, or are actively sharing talent to deploy skills across the organization more fluidly. Eventually, HR profes- sionals must be able to position their product as a solution to a burning business and employee need. So, how are HR's products evolving?

It is safe to say that the pivot to skills as the currency of work requires a wholesale change in HR's product architecture. Our friend and colleague Paul Habgood developed the maturity matrix of HR solutions and practices depicted in figure 6.1, which perfectly captures the evolution required to enable the skills-powered organization. Let's explore each solution in turn.

Workforce Planning	Headcount Planning	Role-Based Planning	Skills Planning	Integrated Capability and Economic Planning
Learning and Development	Job-Based	Skill and Career	Learning in Flow of Work	Perpetual Reinvention
Skills Supply Chain	Hire for Jobs No Contingent Management	Hire for Skills Contingent Procurement	Hire for Skills Total Talent Management	Blended Skills Hiring and Learning
Talent Mobility	Position-Based Mobility	Secondments	Internal Talent Marketplace	Talent Resourcing
Careers	Vertical Careers	Vertical and Horizontal Careers	Careers-Based on Skills	Careers Inside and Outside: Experiences
Organization Design	Static Hierarchy	Flattened Hierarchy	Capability-Based	Network of Teams
Resource Decision Management	My Team (Build or Buy)	My Organisation (Build, Buy or Borrow)	My Company (Build, Buy, Borrow incl. Gig)	Build, Buy, Borrow. Gig. Alliances
Reward and Recognition	Job-Based Reward	Segmented Reward Strategy	Skills-Influenced Reward Decisions	Pay for Skills and Contribution
Work Design	Job-Based	Work Redesign	Task-Level Reinvention	Intelligent Workflows

Alignment of HR solutions with the maturity of your skills data

Skill Data Maturity	No/Minimal Skills Data	Skills Taxonomy Applied to Job Architectures	Workforce Skills and Career Aspirations	AI continuously updating Skills Ontology and Workforce Skills

Figure 6.1
How HR products evolve as skills maturity increases

Workforce planning: With its traditional grounding in jobs, this core process has traditionally been about headcount planning as talent moves from one job to another during a career. The first step in its evolution is to move to role-based planning, which starts to shine a spotlight on the bundle of skills required for each role and the available supply, with the next step being to move to planning at the individual skills level. The most mature state of workforce planning would see it evolve into an integrated capability and economic planning process integrally woven into the organization's strategic planning process.

Learning and development: As previously discussed, this process is viewed as separate from the work, typically job based and grounded in its core technical requirements. The first phase of its evolution is to move to a broader (and more focused) perspective of developing the skills demanded and aligning development to the career aspirations of talent. A more evolved state would see learning and development seamlessly integrated into the flow of work, while the most mature state would see a mindset and toolset that enables the perpetual reinvention of talent as the business itself is being reinvented to meet evolving demand.

Skills supply chain: This has traditionally been defined by the acquisition of employees into jobs from outside the organization. An evolved state would include the acquisition of skills across both employees and contingent labor. A more mature state would involve talent management across every facet of the work relationship (employees in fixed roles and agile talent pools, gig workers, outsourced labor, shared services, etc.). In contrast, the most mature state would integrate skills acquisition, development, and deployment.

Talent mobility: This has traditionally been defined as a position-based movement as talent is moved from one job to another largely permanently. A more mature state typically involves active use of secondments to enable talent to express their skills or acquire skills in different domains. A more evolved state would involve a talent marketplace that enables a plurality of means for talent and skills to be connected to work in the form of gigs, projects, assignments, or jobs. The most mature state would see a holistic approach to talent resourcing leverages a marketplace. This allows for the continuous processing of varying signals of evolving demand for skills, continuous snapshots of the supply of skills and the interest of talent, and seamless matching of supply and demand using all possible work engagement options.

Careers: The earliest iteration of career management involved a singular focus on "moving upwards" in a traditional corporate hierarchy based on jobs. A more mature state involved the notion of "career lattices" and the combination of both lateral and vertical movement, still within the confines of a job. The next iteration involves a skills-powered approach focused on development and skill acquisition through various means within the organization. The most mature state involves a boundaryless career, combining experiences within and outside the organization.

Organization design: The traditional job-based model, with its static hierarchy, is the basic starting point for every organization. A more evolved state involves a more flattened structure with greater agility and autonomy for talent. A more mature state involves the design of a capability-based organization that reflects the different imperatives for various bodies of work. Recall our fixed, flex, and flow models and the shifting imperatives from control to capacity management to capability deployment. The final state involves the ultimate manifestation of the flow model with a network of teams that form and disband as demand and supply for skills evolve.

Resource decision management: Consistent with the traditional hierarchical, job-based construct, the starting point for managing resources is a rather narrow focus on the immediate team and developing team members or acquiring new talent. A more evolved state might consider the broader organization within which multiple teams might sit and the additional option of borrowing talent from other teams. An even more evolved state would consider the entire company and the different ways work could be resourced, including internal gigs and shared services, in addition to the more traditional approaches of building, buying, and borrowing talent. The most mature state would consider all the resources available through an open ecosystem that includes alliances, outsourcing, and other nonemployee options.

Rewards and recognition: Consistent with the currency underpinning the other products, the job is the basic starting point as it relates to the primary currency of rewards and recognition, applied through a more traditional one-size-fits-all approach. A more evolved state would involve segmenting rewards based on the unique supply and demand needs of various roles. A more mature state would involve adjusting rewards and recognition based on acquiring and expressing skills that are pivotal to the business and/or reflect the nature of supply in the market. For the most mature state, recall our case study of the data scientists at the insurance company and the direct link between rewards and the expression of acquired skills and their impact on the business as defined by the contribution of individuals and teams.

Work design: As discussed in chapter 4, work design is a pivotal capability for driving the skills-powered organization. At its most basic level, this would involve the design of jobs, while a more evolved state would involve the design of work beyond jobs to include projects and gigs. A more mature state would involve the deconstruction of jobs, the redistribution of tasks to various work options, and the reconstruction of new ways of working. The most mature state would involve intelligent workflows where work is continuously redesigned based on evolving signals of demand and supply of various work options and skills.

Skills data maturity: This maturity map is in no small part driven by the organization's skills data maturity. Most organizations start with minimal to no skills data given their focus on jobs and jobholders. A more evolved state sees companies developing a skills taxonomy and mapping skills to their job architectures. In contrast, an even more evolved state sees the capturing of workforce skills data and career aspirations at the individual level. The most mature state involves using AI to infer the workforce's evolving skills, updating individual skills profiles and continuously updating skills taxonomies as new skills emerge and legacy ones are rendered obsolete. We will discuss the criticality of data in powering the evolution of the HR function at Standard Chartered shortly.

Enabling and Shaping the Work Experience

The pandemic has been a moment of reckoning for the HR function across the globe—CHROs and HR teams steered the ship with CEOs and leaders during the crisis, making sense of the chaos. As companies prioritize the well-being of their workforces, there is growing recognition of the role of talent as a critical stakeholder group, just like customers, shareholders, and communities increasing the impetus for the evolution of the function, as we have discussed. As more organizations confront the critical need to balance the needs of both the business and the workforce, many acknowledge the opportunity for employee/talent advocacy to be a real force for good. To drive a great client experience, we must first create a great work experience. Managing the work experience requires a level of employee advocacy that few organizations practice. It has been long established that the customer experience is pivotal to driving customer loyalty. Relatively more recent research shows that companies that perform well on work experience metrics also tend to perform well on their customer experience.[2] Additionally, it has found that companies with a more engaged workforce are more profitable than those with poor engagement.[3] This suggests that work experience is critical to driving the productivity that every organization seeks.

The work experience is an amalgamation of all the interactions that talent has with an organization, including relationships with leaders and colleagues, technology, the physical work environment, the design of work, and how talent is developed and deployed. As you can see, delivering on the experience requires partnership and collaboration between HR, other functions, managers, and business leaders. Creating a single, consistent, inclusive experience is certainly not an easy ask! Talent doesn't care if HR, IT, or their manager owns a particular process or part of the experience. They only care that each facet or touchpoint of the experience makes them feel that they belong at the organization. So, while HR may not entirely own the work experience, it has a pivotal role to play in orchestrating it.

At the heart of enabling a best-in-class experience through stronger talent advocacy is the need for active, continuous listening to the voice of all talent and cocreating the experience with them in an inclusive manner. Democratizing access to information and cocreating solutions are core principles that HR functions need to adopt to drive the skills-powered organization.

Being Obsessively Data Driven

As discussed in our discussion about HR's products, data and its effective management are critical to the skills-powered organization. HR professionals need to become fluent at leveraging multiple data sources (employee insights, business, customer trends, HR transactions, etc.), making sense of it, connecting them up to generate differentiated insights, and telling a compelling story to drive decision-making and motivate behavior change. They need to be able to leverage data and analytics to shape conversations with boards, management teams, and people leaders, especially to detail the business case for investments in the workforce and work experience.

The traditional consulting and influencing skills of the function need to be increasingly grounded in the bedrock of data. This will be essential to dealing with the urgent needs of upskilling/ reskilling, skills mobility, and skills-powered deployment. HR must have the data and insights to articulate the commercial case underpinning these critical needs. Further, the function needs to leverage data and analytics to enable the hyperpersonalization and segmentation that is increasingly demanded by the workforce. Research estimates that generative AI could disrupt the equivalent of three hundred million full-time jobs globally,[4] and almost 40 percent of working hours across industries could be impacted by large language models.[5] Generative AI will substitute many skills and augment even more. HR will need the data and insights to enable the business to understand, deploy, and combine human and machine capabilities at scale and speed, delivering on its shifting mandate from being a steward of employment to a steward of work.

Transforming the HR Function at Standard Chartered

The HR team at Standard Chartered has been on a transformational journey as it builds a data-driven function to drive greater impact for the business. The leadership team understood early on the importance of evidence-based decision-making to address business challenges and opportunities, the need to use employee insights to enable a market-leading experience and to achieve the cultural aspirations, and the opportunity that data provides in driving efficient and effective HR operational processes.

As a first step, a specialized People Insights and Analytics (PIA) team was set up, with the skills to pivot from traditional operational reporting to providing strategic insights (and eventually foresight) to support the opportunities and challenges around people, performance, and the future of work. The vision for this team was to unlock value from data so that the HR function could drive more impactful outcomes both economically and culturally. Its offering was clear—going beyond reporting to insights and analytics, specifically focusing on strategic workforce planning. The team started with a focus on the workforce's size and shape with the long-term goal of understanding the skills and investment attached to the future workforce.

At the same time, to generate higher-quality insights and to challenge and provoke discussion using data, significant upskilling was prioritized across the entire HR function. This was to build both confidence and competence in being a data-centric function. In addition to improving their ability to use the data and insights already available, HR teams are getting better equipped to spot value-adding opportunities, resulting in more data-savvy requests for the PIA team. Being able to ground insights and analytics requirements in business problems ensures that the focus is not narrowly on HR data but on broader business data. In 2023, the function embarked on a data fluency learning pathway, a bespoke program designed internally for all colleagues across the function. It is a blend of self-paced learning and facilitator-led sessions, covering a range of topics from the fundamental concepts of data, to building an understanding of existing insights and analytics products, to learning how to connect data to business problems and shape compelling narratives. HR team members completing these learning modules receive a "Data Wizard" badge!

While the entire function has been upskilling to partner effectively with the PIA team, the team itself is also continually upskilling. As part of the journey, the team needed to possess technical skills (such as advanced data analytics) and build human skills such as collaboration and a strong change management mindset. It has been important for the team to prioritize work based on the value that can be derived from it. This means investing time at the beginning of an insights request with stakeholders (HR colleagues as well as business leaders) to understand the challenge (or opportunity) at hand, to estimate the work's ROI, and to identify how to track whether a particular piece of work has been effective and delivered the intended outcomes. The work doesn't end when the PIA team has produced a report and shared the insights—it only ends when the predefined measures of success are achieved. And even after a project is completed, it is about ensuring that these use cases are appropriately showcased to raise awareness of the "art of the possible," which happens via regular function-wide newsletters. For PIA team members to be able to spend valuable time with colleagues across teams and markets, it has had to automate reporting to the greatest extent possible. Substituting this repetitive, mundane work has allowed the team's time and capacity to be repurposed into "insight partner" work, enabling it to engage with HR colleagues to better understand the blockers to strong data-centricity, define key data requirements, and provide advisory services around business and workforce needs. From an operational perspective, this has also resulted in refining the number of reports generated (from approximately eight thousand previously to just one thousand today), enabling focus of the reporting engine on the biggest commercial challenges and opportunities.

Having improved the quality of insights for driving better business outcomes, the next step for the HR function was to democratize access to data, insights, and analytics to deliver impact at scale. This started with providing the right access and tools to HR colleagues and then further putting insights into the hands of the end users, supported by the right technology to make the experience highly intuitive. A foundational example is the annual employee sentiment survey results and the survey results for "moments that matter" such as onboarding and exit. The survey results dashboards were first made accessible to all HR colleagues so that the data was uniformly available for them to use in conversations with stakeholders and when designing and deploying HR products and interventions (such as performance management, employee well-being, and learning and development). The enterprise-wide results for the annual employee survey were then made accessible to all people leaders, with a substantive view of the data now made accessible to all employees. This is enabling not just greater transparency but also the sharing of best practices across leaders and teams throughout the organization.

A journey that began with the goal of encouraging colleagues to become comfortable with data self-service, and shifting the mindset that only a specialized team can provide analytics, has led to a significant number of HR professionals building new skills to work with a suite of reports and dashboards to generate their insights and recommendations from the data available. As a data-driven HR function, the aspiration is for everyone to be able to ask the right questions and be equipped to answer them in ways that are descriptive (i.e., what happened in the past), diagnostic (i.e., why something happened), predictive (i.e., what is most likely to happen in the future), and prescriptive (i.e., what recommended actions are needed to achieve the desired outcomes). This is because being data led is about understanding, interpreting, and using data effectively in various HR roles. For example, it means being able to undertake a deep dive into talent attrition data, not just focusing on trends for a part of the business but also identifying the drivers behind the attrition and the impact this has on sunset/ sunrise roles, on the skills needed to deliver strategic outcomes, or on the diversity of various talent pools. It also means being capable of ascertaining projections of future attrition to drive the decisions required to address the loss of talent when it has a high impact on business delivery.

Fostering greater awareness of, and encouraging active advocacy to build, this data-driven culture started at the top—with the CHRO and HR leadership team. Setting the tone has been important, and it has been even more powerful to have senior leaders role model the use of data and lean into shaping the insights they need to have insightful and impactful conversations with business leaders and peers. For example, data and analytics play a key role in the CHRO's ongoing conversations with the board and global management team on how best to deploy human capital. Every quarter, the CHRO takes a "People Insights" presentation to the global management team, which captures trends and insights on key people priorities and risk pillars (workforce size; shape of the firm; productivity, capability, and skills; performance; and potential and state of the culture) to highlight areas of focus and action. These range from organizational effectiveness actions such as adjusting the spans of control that people leaders are operating with and the layers of structural hierarchy in different teams to rethinking the quantity and nature of learning being consumed by employees in sunrise and sunset roles. During the COVID-19 pandemic, this presentation was supplemented with specific data points on employee stress, time off, and well-being to enable decision-making and action via direct messages to the workforce and other interventions. This has set the tone for all leaders that their teams are expected to engage actively with PIA colleagues on relevant use cases and ensure that action is taken based on the insights being generated.

Progress continues to be made in strengthening the underlying fundamentals needed for a data-driven function. The HR teams continue to work on options to enable a seamless, automated integration of data derived from across their suite of various HR technology products (such as from their HR information system, employee survey tools, internal talent marketplace, feedback exchange tools) to eventually support an interconnected insights narrative and a more enhanced user experience (for both HR colleagues and business stakeholders). This requires maintaining a robust data architecture to support speed of insight, democratization of access and self-service, and the strategic management of HR data to optimize value creation in line with data governance, data privacy, and responsible AI.

As Standard Chartered's HR function evolves its role and product suite to transform the work experience to enable a skills-powered organization, data and analytics have been, and continue to be, pivotal to its journey.

7 Beyond the Organization

As shown throughout this book, the traditional "closed" work operating system, which uses jobs as its basic currency with limited permutations and variations, is increasingly insufficient for delivering the resilience, agility, or flexibility required by twenty-first-century organizations and workforces. As we move into an era where skills are the currency of work, you see the quantum gains possible if we can unlearn the routines, logic, and disciplines that have shaped 140 years of work. You also start to see how a skills-powered organization is better equipped to access various work options, both within and outside the organization, operating in a more open and inclusive ecosystem.

As we discussed in the introduction, companies have been moving work outside their organizational boundaries for many years now. However, as we evolve our thinking beyond the notion of a job to skills, we significantly reduce the frictional cost of tapping talent outside the organization. By using skills as the currency of work, companies can transform a traditional B2B relationship (i.e., one between an organization and a third party, like an outsourcer or managed services provider whereby entire jobs might be "lifted and shifted") to a B2C relationship (i.e., a relationship between an organization and individual gig workers, typically powered through an external talent marketplace whereby specific tasks are matched to a gig worker's skills), increasing the efficiency and effectiveness with which external talent can be engaged with the organization's work.

As companies open the aperture of thinking about the free flow of work and talent across traditional boundaries, as described by Arthur Yeung and Dave Ulrich in their book *Reinventing the Organization: How Companies Can Deliver Radically Greater Value in Fast-Changing Markets*, we start to see many new players emerge as capabilities and skills are shared and rented.[1] Governments, nongovernmental organizations, unions, service providers, talent platforms, educational institutions, and even competitors become partners in sharing the risks and benefits of growth and innovation. The resurgence of the labor movement in many countries is a reflection of the need for a more balanced and equitable mechanism for sharing value between different stakeholders. As skills become the currency of work, not only do we see the emergence of new organization structures powered by the emerging technologies underlying Web3, but we also see opportunities for governments to participate in ensuring a sufficient supply of skills more actively through frequent and rapid upskilling and reskilling of their populations and the creation of funding mechanisms that democratize access to learning and development. In this chapter, we explore how organizational forms are morphing to enable more open ecosystems with emerging technologies as well as how the governments of two countries are providing the funding, infrastructure, and processes to support the development and deployment of skills at scale and pace.

Communities as a Critical Element of the New Work Operating Model

Think back to our discussion about the evolution of work beyond the traditional industrial model that underpinned the Second Industrial Revolution. As we have moved into the Third and Fourth Industrial Revolutions, work and talent have progressively fled their traditional structural boundaries. As Leena Nair, then CHRO of Unilever and now CEO of Chanel, once infamously said at the 2020 World Economic Forum Annual Meeting in Davos that "culture is the new structure." Culture is the thing that binds disparate interests to a common mission and purpose in a way that traditional organization design, with its hierarchies and control systems, tried to but never really could. Our friend and colleague Gary Bolles recently said that "the age of the industrial-era organization is coming to an end. In its place: The Age of the Organization as Community" in an article on LinkedIn.[2] He goes on to describe the two key elements underpinning community as identity (i.e., the members have something in common like geography or an interest) and membership, which often isn't binary. For example, you might be part of one community 100 percent of the time (like a job) and part of another for 5 percent of your time (like your freelance gig).

Technology, particularly Web3, is further accelerating this shift to communities in the form of DAOs.[3] DAOs exploit smart contract architectures and digital tokens verified on public blockchains, such as Ethereum, to give members of a DAO the possibility to participate directly in its governance and its work. Decision-making thus becomes collective and based on how many votes—expressed in the number of tokens—a certain proposal in the DAO gets. There are no barriers to entry, and owning tokens in a DAO is permissionless. Since all rules are coded in smart contracts, and all transactions are recorded on a blockchain, a DAO is fully transparent to its members. If the DAO is purposed with developing ideas or software, then the intellectual property is open sourced, at least for now.

As DAOs are adopted more widely, new types of businesses will emerge that would look more like cooperatives and less like traditional corporations, significantly reducing agency costs. In such decentralized organizations, leadership will rely on soft power and empathy, using culture and shared values to align the interests and skills of disparate stakeholders to a common mission and purpose.

In a DAO, there are no officers, directors, or managers. Leadership roles are more fluid and impermanent, giving more opportunities to members to contribute based on their unique skills. DAOs may decide to prioritize social goods—such as job security—above operational efficiency. This shift from hierarchical structures to flat, widely distributed networks and ecosystems run by stakeholder communities instead of boards and executives will also have a profound impact on work. The table below illustrates the fundamental differences between traditional organizations and DAOs.

Features	Traditional organization	DAO
Decision-making	Centralized	Collective
Ownership	Permissioned	Permissionless
Structure	Hierarchical	Flat/distributed
Information Flows	Private and gated	Transparent and public
Intellectual Property	Closed-sourced	Open-sourced

Source: Ben Schecter, "The Future of Work Is Not Corporate—It's DAOs and and Crypto Networks,"a16z crypto, December 17, 2021, https://a16zcrypto.com/posts/article/the-future-of-work-daos-crypto-networks/.

In chapter 2, we explored the three models for connecting talent to work (fixed, flex, and flow) with skills as the currency of work for companies organized within the context of a more traditional corporate structure. With the introduction of DAOs, we see the possibility for a fourth option with even less friction and much greater agility, one where work flows to talent. Figure 7.1 illustrates these four models.

Within the context of work being organized as DAOs, the traditional hierarchical mix of roles within a corporate structure (leader, manager, employee, contractor, and vendor) and functions will morph significantly into a flatter construct comprising the following:

- A core group of individuals responsible for coordinating work and delivering on the DAO's value proposition
- A broader contributor group that provides specific services to execute the DAO's mission, which includes other DAOs that provide services like HR, finance, accounting, and customer service on an ongoing basis and individual contributors (gig workers or contractors) who take on projects as needed
- An even broader group of "members" who will promote brands, support continued crowdsourcing of ongoing product innovation, or otherwise contribute to the advancement of the DAO's mission

Each of these groups will be rewarded quite differently. The core group will share in the total value created by the DAO less payments to the other two groups. The payments to the contributor group will vary between fixed payments for ongoing services in the case of a DAO providing HR services and more episodic payments to individual contributors as they take on and execute specific projects. Members will be rewarded as they make various contributions to the DAO, with the potential for payment in nonfungible tokens with virtual-to-physical redemptions.

Today, in most places around the world, DAOs do not have a legal status, which poses serious issues, especially when a DAO extends its activities beyond the digital space. Regulators are still struggling to keep up with the high rate of innovation that comes from Web3 pioneers. Nevertheless, there are already clear opportunities for businesses to start thinking and piloting use cases for a decentralized future. Here are a few ways to prototype your initial steps into this new world of work flowing to talent:

- Broaden the participation in your business model. DAOs present us with an opportunity to increase the enterprise's agility by enabling work to

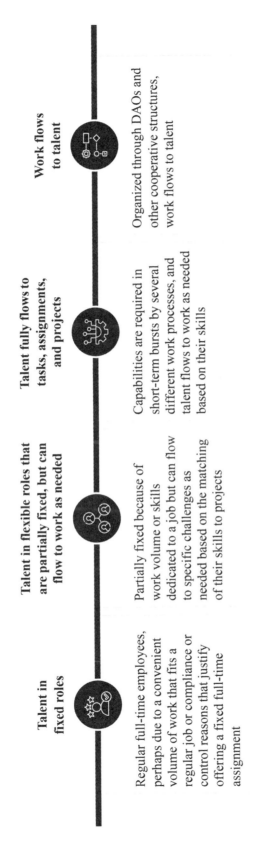

Talent in fixed roles

Regular full-time employees, perhaps due to a convenient volume of work that fits a regular job or compliance or control reasons that justify offering a fixed full-time assignment

Talent in flexible roles that are partially fixed, but can flow to work as needed

Partially fixed because of work volume or skills dedicated to a job but can flow to specific challenges as needed based on the matching of their skills to projects

Talent fully flows to tasks, assignments, and projects

Capabilities are required in short-term bursts by several different work processes, and talent flows to work as needed based on their skills

Work flows to talent

Organized through DAOs and other cooperative structures, work flows to talent

Figure 7.1

Beyond the organization. *Source:* Ravin Jesuthasan. Adapted from Ravin Jesuthasan and John Boudreau, "Work without Jobs," *Sloan Management Review,* January 5, 2021.

flow to talent beyond the traditional walls of the organization, using skills as the currency for connecting this distributed enterprise. Consider creating a DAO that enables the broader community of stakeholders in your business to participate in promoting your brands or crowdsourcing ideas for innovation to access a broader ecosystem of skills.

- Consider using blockchain token rewards to incentivize freelancers, remote contract workers, and other types of nonemployee labor working on projects and gigs. This will enable you to reward high performers for their direct contributions to the execution of your business model.

- Experiment with taking the idea of a DAO further by outsourcing environmental, social, and corporate goals to a DAO governed by your company's stakeholders, such as employees, contractors, suppliers, and impacted communities.

- Identify opportunities and use cases in your core processes where the gradual transition to a blockchain-enabled future will add value, and include them in your digital transformation agenda.

As you can see, DAOs present us with some unique opportunities to reinvent the organization beyond its traditional boundaries. Let's turn our attention to how other stakeholders, particularly governments, are supporting and enabling open skills-powered ecosystems.

As we have discussed in the introduction, one of the great benefits of making skills the currency of the labor market (instead of jobs) is the opportunity to connect more talent to work beyond just those with degrees. In the United States, 60 percent of workers don't have a four-year college degree, yet US employers have made these degrees prerequisites even to be considered for most new jobs paying a middle-class wage or better. A research report by Opportunity@Work and Accenture identified a talent pool of seventy-one million workers who are Skilled Through Alternative Routes (STARs).[4] These are individuals who have developed critical foundational and behavioral skills through their civilian or military work experience. Millions more acquired technical and functional skills in community college, last-mile training programs, or on the job:

- Five million STARs (Shining STARs) currently work in high-wage jobs today despite the barriers to entry they face. Shining STARs are proof of what is possible.

- Thirty million STARs (Rising STARs) currently work in jobs with skill requirements, suggesting they can perform a job in the next highest wage category. They have the skills and potential today to see transformative wage gains of more than 70 percent, on average.
- Thirty-six million STARs (Forming STARs) have skills for occupations paying at least 10 percent higher than their current jobs but are not well situated for job transitions that would provide transformative wage gains. Low-wage Forming STARs are especially susceptible to the impact of automation.

So, how can communities around the world create the opportunities for everyone to both acquire and express the skills needed to thrive in the new world of work? Let's explore how two progressive governments are supporting talent and companies by creating the structures needed to drive a skills-powered economy.

Singapore SkillsFuture

Singapore is taking a skills-first approach to preparing its workforce of the future by anticipating the skills needed by the market and encouraging citizens to gain those skills to increase employment and productivity.[5] And at the same time, they are engaging employers to adopt skills-powered hiring and career development for their employees. This effort is being led by SkillsFuture Singapore Agency (SSG), which focuses on providing Singaporeans with lifelong learning through reskilling and upskilling opportunities for a more competitive economy. SSG provides resources such as SkillsFuture Credit, Jobs-Skills Insights, Skills and Training Advisory services, and the MySkillsFuture online portal to empower Singaporeans to chart their career and lifelong learning pathways. SkillsFuture Credit, funded by the Singapore government, provides financial support for training to Singaporeans. The credits are distributed to eligible individuals through their dedicated SkillsFuture Credit account via the MySkillsFuture online portal, through which they can access using their Singpass (a citizen's unique digital identity used for all secure transactions). The credits are currently distributed to citizens based on their age.

Since SkillsFuture Credit was introduced in 2015, the participation rate for skill development has increased from 35 percent in 2015 to 50 percent in 2022. While research is ongoing regarding its long-term impact, initial responses indicate positive outcomes. In 2021, 94 percent of the surveyed trainees indicated that they could perform better at work after undergoing SSG-funded training. Over a five-year period (from 2016 to 2021), the number of Singaporeans who have used their SkillsFuture Credits nearly doubled, from 126,000 in 2016 to 247,000 in 2021. SSG is continuing to expand access as it believes that everyone in the workforce should continue to pursue reskilling at the workplace and via institutional-based learning. The experience of Singapore shows that governments and policymakers can be the "convenor" of a broad and open ecosystem, supporting companies, educational institutions, and other partners in the skills ecosystem and managing the skills demand and supply to develop and sustain a competitive and inclusive economy.

France's Skills Investment Plan

Initiated in 2018, this plan targets three objectives, while also focusing on the implementation of a pilot project or national reform.[6]

1. Training for one million low-skilled/unskilled jobseekers and one million young people furthest away from the labor market, in particular people with disabilities and those living in select urban and rural priority neighborhoods
2. Meeting the needs of companies facing recruiting difficulties
3. Contributing to the changing demand for skills, particularly in digital and green transitions

The program has a national scope but is implemented on a regional scale (by regional councils) as part of the regional Skills Investment Pacts. These pacts are the territorial expression of the Skills Investment Plan, considering the specificities of each region. To ensure France's sustainable growth, the investment is allocated in the following ways:

- Accelerating the green transition (€20 billion)
- Building a society of skills (€15 billion)
- Increasing competitiveness through innovation (€13 billion)
- Building digital capabilities (€9 billion)

The plan has been successful in moving the needle on upskilling and reskilling, with training being provided to 964,000 job seekers in 2019. The access rate to training for the least qualified job seekers increased in 2019 (10 percent, compared to 8.4 percent in 2018). To promote higher access rates for them, the plan introduced new national preparatory programs to better equip them before entering training courses. Senior job seekers and adults (twenty-six to forty-four years) have benefited the most from this plan. Their access rates rose sharply, especially in 2019. The access rate of youth looking for work remained stable, at around 16 to 17 percent.

In addition, like Singapore, France also has developed personal training accounts for its citizens.[7] Every citizen who works either part or full time receives €500 per year of work up to a €5,000 maximum, and the amounts are not subject to income tax. There is also a provision for an employer contribution, which increases the amount available for upskilling/reskilling.

Programs like these in Singapore and France are growing rapidly as more governments recognize the need for frictionless mechanisms that allow their citizens to upskill and reskill quickly and frequently, allowing them to (re)deploy their skills across many organizations over time.

Let's explore how Standard Chartered is thinking about its broader ecosystem beyond the traditional boundaries of the organization.

Driving Skill Building across Communities at Standard Chartered

A global and collective effort will be needed to accelerate progress toward the United Nations Sustainable Development Goal (UNSDG) 8 to "achieve full and productive employment, and decent work, for all women and men by 2030." The COVID-19 pandemic, climate change, and various conflicts have continued to exacerbate the problems of inequality, and changes to the labor market have had a disproportionate impact on marginalized groups across communities, especially among young people, women, and people with disabilities. Given the expected impact of the Fourth Industrial Revolution in disrupting work and jobs (as highlighted in the introduction), there is a real danger that the gap between education and employability will continue to grow wider. This would lead to unemployment challenges and significant societal impacts. There is an even higher risk for those without specialized skills, who are often from vulnerable populations that are starting from a lower baseline and are expected to be more adversely impacted than before, and thus fall even further behind. The choices made by business leaders, policymakers, education providers, workers, and learners today will shape economies for generations to come. It is more important than ever for all stakeholders to come together, listen to those most affected, and identify solutions to enable the next generation to thrive, making collective efforts and investments.

Standard Chartered strongly believes that a concerted effort between governments, multilateral institutions, and responsible corporations is required to ensure meaningful and sustainable progress toward UNSDG 8. The role of business in helping bridge the gap between education and employability, and in providing reskilling opportunities at scale for the wider communities within which it operates, is an area of deep interest to its senior leaders. In 2019, the Futuremakers program was launched to leverage its expertise as a bank and work through staff volunteering and local partners to help the next generation learn, earn, and grow. Through the program, the firm has been supporting disadvantaged young people to learn new skills and to enhance employability and enable entrepreneurship. For example, it provides vocational training, mentoring, career planning, upskilling, and reskilling opportunities that support young people in becoming "work ready." It also provides them with support to develop broader business skills, build financial knowledge, and gain access to finance and social networks. The program has reached more than one million young people (74 percent young women) between 2019 and 2022 across forty-three markets.

Mirroring its commitment to workplace inclusion, it strongly believes in the power of investing in girls, understanding that this can lead to increased prosperity and diversity. Giving girls the tools to shape their own future is seen as having an incredible multiplier effect on communities and societies, and therefore they have been a key focus for its efforts. Through a dedicated program called Goal, the focus has been on equipping adolescent girls with the skills, knowledge, and confidence needed to be economic leaders in their families and communities. For example, using sport- and activity-based learning, they deliver learning modules on financial education and communication skills. Their Women in Tech initiative further provides technical business training, mentoring, and seed funding to women entrepreneurs.

While these bespoke programs have been incredibly successful, the organization is envisioning further scaling the reach it has on skill building in its ecosystem by leveraging technology to deploy an approach that is future focused, perpetual, and systemic. It is exploring building a reskilling mobile application (in collaboration with a third-party vendor) that could extend impact by enabling learning, skill building, and career opportunity exploration for clients and communities. The app could also provide access to a range of bite-sized, easy-to-consume content, especially around future-focused topics where the firm has unique expertise to offer, such as through their core expertise at the intersection of digital and banking or through their experience in embedding sustainability across their business. It could also enable access to topical community and discussion forums and the opportunity to connect with subject matter experts or even other app users. Moreover, the app could include features such as a diagnostic assessment, which could help users reflect on their values and experiences so that they can better understand their own career possibilities and, in turn, their priorities and goals as a learner.

To convert this skill building into employment opportunities, the app could then include a link to the Standard Chartered hiring portal as well as access to employee stories and "spotlight" careers. The plan would be to initially target professionals and the "hidden workforce" who are looking for a career change. As the app would evolve, there could be opportunity to explore expanding access to more targeted segments such as young adults preparing to join the workforce and those who are being supported through other existing initiatives (such as its Futuremakers and Goal programs).

8 A Guide to Becoming a Skills-Powered Organization and Thriving in a Skills-Powered World

Let's start with a quick recap of our journey to build the case for, define, illustrate, and otherwise bring to life the skills-powered organization. Over the last five years, more organizations and governments have come to recognize the power of having skills as the currency of work and the labor market. However, reversing 140 years of the legacy of jobs will require time and focused effort. An increasing array of work either has already shifted (such as the tasks now posted to internal talent marketplaces or tasks obtained through freelance platforms), will soon shift (such as work that is being combined with automation, work that has become remote, or where traditional job descriptions have a short half-life), or *should* shift to being skills powered (such as work where it is difficult to find qualified workers, where development and career paths seem stuck, or where there is pressure to offshore or outsource).

We started off with a discussion of the evolution of work and the case for the skills-powered organization. We then defined it and explored the critical capabilities required to lead it. In chapter 2 we explored how work might be organized in the skills-powered organization and the three models for connecting talent to work. We then shifted our experience to discussing what the work experience looked like and the pivotal role of learning in shaping the overall talent value proposition. In chapter 4 we discussed the critical capabilities underpinning the skills-powered organization as we delved into work design, development, and deployment. The essential role of AI in powering the organization was our next topic of exploration as we discussed the capabilities of various platforms. We shifted our attention to discussing the HR function in chapter 6, exploring the evolution of its service architecture and role. In chapter 7 we turned our attention beyond the traditional walls of the organization to understand how the broader ecosystem of work is enhanced by making skills its currency. And we brought all the theory and practice to life through the real-world experiences at Standard Chartered.

We conclude with a guide for how you as a leader might get started on the journey to becoming a skills-powered organization and discuss how you as an individual or your children can thrive in a skills-powered world.

Getting Your Organization Started on the Journey

While it might seem like an insurmountable challenge to get your organization and its leaders thinking about, let alone operating and leading, a skills-powered organization, we have seen many organizations embark on the journey and realize the expected benefits. In our experience, there are three critical factors that must be addressed:

1. Establish a North Star to anchor your journey
2. Experiment, experiment, experiment
3. Focus on the key enablers of success

Let's explore each of these in turn.

Establish a North Star

So, what do we mean by a North Star? It is

- a clear statement about your vision to guide your direction and program of work to becoming a skills-powered organization
- simple and enduring—it is your touchstone to ensure you remain on track
- one big idea (not five in one)
- clearly aligned to addressing specific business needs
- a clear definition of the outcomes you expect to accomplish by embarking on the journey to being a skills-powered organization

Figure 8.1 is a generic North Star that should help you get started with yours. As you can see, it begins with its vision and target outcomes, clearly defines what it looks like and what it feels like and the critical foundations that underpin it.

Microsoft is viewed as a leader on the journey to becoming a skills-powered organization. It has consistently used a North Star and its various components to guide its journey. At the end of 2023, we had an opportunity to speak with Karen Kocher, global leader of Microsoft HR's Future of Work, about her work. Karen describes the importance and role of a North Star as follows: "Microsoft very much believes in anchoring its future aspirations and activities in North Star components such as vision statements, strategies, and measurable outcomes. These North Star elements form an excellent context in which future building such as signal gathering, scenario planning, and experimentation can occur in a more focused and informative way. North Star components are important to narrow the aperture somewhat, providing the team with clarity, while continuing to facilitate the broad and diverse thinking necessary for the team to take early action to learn and build." Karen goes on to describe how Microsoft's North Star has shaped their journey: "The envisioning we've done on the Future of Work and our Skills strategy is more focused and efficient because we put in place key elements of a North Star early on. These help establish transparency and direction while we continue to search for answers to questions through means of experimentation."

While many tend to focus on aligning initiatives to a North Star, it is an equally powerful tool to determine what initiatives should not be pursued. "Simple, clear North Star content helps provide a touchstone of sorts for all those working on the initiative and those that are connected," Karen explains. She continues: "As signals and ideas come in and experimentation opportunities evolve, next step possibilities arise, and the team can then much more effectively discuss what's in and what's out. Being able to focus on what's important while pushing aside what isn't helps the team continue forward momentum while also creating a backlog of items for consideration in the future. The North Star has also shaped how we think about, prioritize, and act on experimentation. We know that we must start somewhere and that early learnings need to come from the opportunities most closely aligned to the outcomes needed. This helps us sift through all the possibilities, be clear on dependencies, and organize possibilities according to an above and below the line prioritization."

Experiment, Experiment, Experiment

We have discussed at length how significant a change it is to become a skills-powered organization and the myriad challenges associated with

WHAT IT LOOKS LIKE

Our systems, processes, policies, and culture will support **organizational agility, continuous learning, and perpetual reinvention.**

A new work model that is optimized for:

1. **The Work:** redesigned to enable talent to flow to it seamlessly whi enabling its perpetual reinvention

2. **The Work Experience:** Re-envisioned talent experience to meet all talent on their terms, rewarding development and contribution while designing in space for learning and well-being

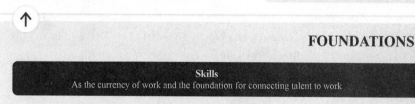

Figure 8.1

North Star: To enable the agile deployment and development of talent with skills as the currency of work increasing productivity, agility, and velocity

moving beyond the legacy of a one-to-one relationship between jobs and jobholders to the many-to-many relationships between skills and work. We have seen through the Standard Chartered examples the power of proto-types and experiments in enabling the shift in mindset, skill set, and tool-set. Experiments are critical for testing and applying the design principles underpinning the skills-powered organization before they are deployed across the organization. But how do you decide which experiments to pursue? Figure 8.2 illustrates the key considerations covering the impact, design, scope, metrics, duration, and scope.

Microsoft is well-known for its thoughtful approach to experimentation and prototyping. Underpinning any North Star should be a set of guiding principles that are used to shape various initiatives and experiments. According to Karen Kocher, "Guiding principles are a fundamental component of most of the work Microsoft does. The guiding principles within

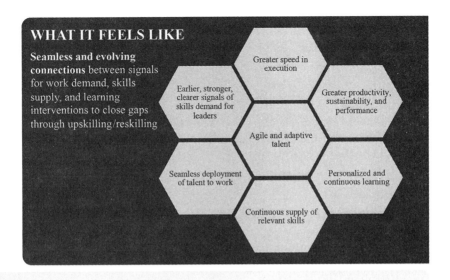

our Future of Work and Skills initiatives have helped us clearly explain priorities. We can more easily decide where to act and what actions to take, and we stay focused on how to work together and what success looks like. The guiding principles anchor experimentation in terms of what to do, when and how to do it, and whether successful trends are realized. Guiding principles are important for providing clear expectations for why an experiment is being done, how it will be conducted, and what everyone can expect at the conclusion."

The following generic guiding principles (figure 8.3) will help you get started. As you can see, the guiding principles start with a clear definition of the objectives that every experiment must address. These objectives help ensure each experiment's sustainability and long-term value creation potential. The principles also define the roles and responsibilities of the various stakeholders involved to ensure proper governance. Last, the success

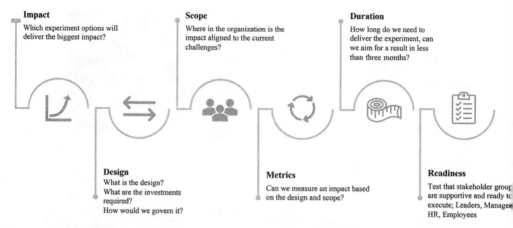

Impact
Which experiment options will deliver the biggest impact?

Scope
Where in the organization is the impact aligned to the current challenges?

Duration
How long do we need to deliver the experiment, can we aim for a result in less than three months?

Design
What is the design?
What are the investments required?
How would we govern it?

Metrics
Can we measure an impact based on the design and scope?

Readiness
Test that stakeholder group are supportive and ready to execute; Leaders, Manager HR, Employees

Figure 8.2
Experiment selection framework: Assessing options for experiment viability alignment to the North Star

metrics expected of each experiment are clearly defined to ensure all stakeholders are clear on the anticipated outcomes.

Focus on the Key Enablers

We have discussed these enablers over the course of chapters 2–6, where we explored the organization and different ways of connecting talent to work, the defining features of the skills-driven work experience, the organization capabilities of work design, development and deployment, the critical role of AI, and the new routines and practices required of the HR function. Let's detail them all here:

1. Leaders
   - Encourage and support the shift in culture and mindset for the new work operating system from jobs and jobholders to skills and work
   - Build capability in redesigning work
   - Be active mentors
   - Make internal mobility part of the culture and operating model
   - Make DEI part of decisions
   - Align incentives and budgets so they are not impediments

OBJECTIVES AND IMPACT

Tangible and measurable objectives of the experiment program:

1. **Inform a long-term, intentional skills strategy** that supports the transition to a more productive, agile, and higher velocity way of working

2. **Inform the development** of additional short-term experiments that work toward a long-term strategy

3. **Test presumed roadblocks** to the implementation of skills initiatives

4. **Collect data** to determine individual, team, and organizational impact

5. **Gather adoption and utilization insights,** to inform change management plans for broader rollout

6. **Collect real usage anecdotes and stories** to share during broader roll-out

7. **Utilizing learnings** to improve designs and solutions of future skills experiments

ROLES AND GOVERNANCE

Program Team:
The program team is responsible for owning the roadmap of skills-related experiments, determining if an experiment qualifies for the program based on its alignment to the skills vision, prioritizing experiments in a strategic cadence, and ensuring experiments have the resources needed to succeed.

←

Experiment Teams:
The purpose of **skills experiment teams** is to support design and implementation of experiments to inform the broader skills strategy.

- What are roles and responsibilities of each team member?
- How does communication flow between the program team, experiment teams, and teams outside the skills network?
- What communication channels are used?

SUCCESS METRICS

☆ Engagement

☆ Work Output (Quality and Quantity)

☆ Time to Productivity

☆ Agility

☆ Cost/Return on Investment

☆ Productivity

☆ Upskilling and Reskilling

☆ Successfully tests potential roadblocks and informs a long-term skills strategy

Figure 8.3
Guiding principles for skills experiments

2. Governance
   - Clearly defined accountability governance for managing and updating the skills taxonomy
   - Global guidelines for talent deployment while accounting for legal/local requirements
   - Accountability for resources decisions—can anyone create demand for work?
   - Who will be responsible for updating and maintaining various policies and protocols?
   - Clear decision rights for contracting, performance management, and measurement
3. Employees
   - Responsible for creating and maintaining their skills profile
   - Proactively engage with opportunities as they emerge (open jobs, projects, and gigs) across the organization
   - Identify skills gaps and development areas
   - Commit to learning high-value adjacent skills and looking for opportunities to express acquired skills
   - Create personal career and developmental plans
4. Culture and change management
   - Creating a culture of skills-powered development and deployment is an enterprise-wide effort
   - Engage all stakeholders and cocreate to build a desirable future
   - Communicate proactively to set expectations, mitigate risk, and promote the change narrative
   - Activate and monitor the work experience across the business to ensure accountability and sustainability
5. HR function
   - Create a center of expertise to support leaders and managers with redesigning work
   - Determine/validate the specific skills required for various types of work
   - Actively align training and career paths to the specific skills required
   - Champion the skills-powered organization by ensuring executive sponsorship and robust change management

- Reenvision and redesign core people processes (performance management, compensation, benefits, talent acquisition, talent assessment, learning and development)
- Help employees with creating and updating their skill profiles
- Support managers in actively using internal talent marketplaces

6. Functional processes, such as finance, IT, and legal
   - Accounting for work being done across boundaries—what finance workflows, accounting, and approvals are needed?
   - Ensure compliance of talent deployment with local market requirements
   - Planning and maintenance of data and the technology stack required to enable the skills-powered organization

7. Technology and AI
   - The optimal combination of technology platforms—do we want skills profiles in more than one place?
   - AI smart matching of skills supply to demand and matching of developmental resources to close skill gaps
   - Data flow and ERP interfaces (core data, learning and career development tools, pay and performance management)
   - User interface for employees, managers, HR professionals, and recruiters
   - Advanced analytics and dashboard (e.g., what is the demand trendline for various skills, and how is the supply of skills trending in meeting demand)

8. Foundational enablers
   - Skills-powered organization of work and work structures
   - Overall skills taxonomy capturing technical and enabling skills
   - Skills validation, such as proficiency levels and skill assessments
   - Skill profiles and mapping of skills to work

While this might seem like a long list of enablers, it is important to remember that this is a journey. Organizations committed to this journey soon experience a "flywheel" effect, where continued experimentation and attention to enablers not only accelerate progress but also enhance organizational commitment and discipline in addressing other enablers.

We have discussed what it takes to drive the skills-powered organization. What about you as an individual or the next generation of talent? How will you thrive in a skills-powered world, and how will you adapt to the new ways of working required? Our friend and colleague Lewis Garrard framed it best with these six tips.[1]

1. **Get clear on your raw material.**

   Who are you? What motivates and interests you? What are your aspirations? Many people make terrible career choices because they overlook the importance of enjoying the actual work and overvalue the potential prestige and accoutrements of the title and position.[2] Many people also get distracted looking for a passion rather than trying to understand what they have the potential and aspiration to be great at.

   To make better decisions, you'll need data about your personality, values, and motivators. Look for well-validated tools to do this or design a short survey to ask 5–10 people who know you well to share 3–6 adjectives that describe you best. Sometimes, the best way to discover yourself is to understand how you appear in the eyes of others.

2. **Do a personal skills audit.**

   Many people have no idea what skills they actually have, or how to benchmark them against others. Part of the problem is that they have no taxonomy or language to describe and signal their skills. To solve this, some organizations are starting to offer tools that help you with skills discovery—using an AI to understand your learning and job history to predict your skills and proficiency levels. For deep technical skills, you might want to use an assessment to get an accurate gauge of your capabilities and proficiencies. If you're already at a large organization, then you may have access to some technologies that can help you with this—like a talent marketplace or learning technology.[3] If you don't have access to one of those, you can either see what LinkedIn[4] has to offer or put the effort in and decide for yourself using an existing skills framework or taxonomy[5] that you can find online.

   The key outcome here is to have a clear list of twenty to thirty skills and their proficiency levels so you can start to see yourself as a bundle of capabilities that can flex and bend to multiple different types of work—and not just one job.

3. **Decide on a strategy—how will you be unique?**

   Hybrid work has become all about where we work—a mix of office and home (or hotel for some!), but perhaps a better way to think about it is the hybridization of the type of work that people do—combining different domains of work to create entire new outcomes. What does that mean? It means that being an HR leader who can code or an engineering leader who can design brand strategy. It means combining skill sets to see problems from an entirely different lens. And it helps to create an idiosyncratic value proposition for every person–allowing them to lean into their strengths. It also increases the opportunities for people to stand out, feel unique, and be seen and valued.

4. **Invest in your skills to build skills.**

No matter what you do, it'll be difficult to know exactly what to learn. Focusing on critical core skills like influence, sense-making, transdisciplinary thinking, and learning strategies build the foundations for staying relevant. In our work, we sometimes call these the "skills to build skills" because they are capabilities that help people work with others, think creatively, and maintain focus on personal growth.[6] They are also relatively difficult to build because they take a lot of practice to get right across a lot of different situations.

So, how can you start to develop these critical core skills? The answer is relatively simple—pay a lot of attention to them. Find people who you see demonstrating them. Watch what they do and ask them questions about how they think. The best way to learn core skills is from effective role models.

5. **Figure out your (in)side hustle.**

One of the best ways to acquire new skills and learn about new directions that you might love to pursue is to participate in projects that expose you to new ideas, people, and problems. This will mean finding ways to take on projects that stretch you outside of your day-to-day assignments. Doing this requires some discipline and a capacity to say no to things that can knock you off track. A concept that is useful is to review a list of all your personal projects and to make judgments about which ones to really invest in, being aware of the conflicts that can sometimes happen between them.[7] It's worth keeping in mind that skills building is often effortful, and it so requires some investment, which will therefore mean you will need to be careful how much you take on.

6. **Assign some value to your culture and organization-specific skills.**

Every organization has a certain way of doing things that is unique. Don't hesitate to build out capabilities that help you accelerate within your organization while being differentiated. The process of figuring out what is unique about an organization as a community, how it operates, and how to get the best from it is a skill in and of itself. Focus on learning ways to identify what makes the particular environment you are in unique and what the equation is for being successful within it. But don't let it blind you, as you will need to apply the same learning and skills to figure out how to be effective if you move to a new organization. The point is that seeing and adapting to context is a skill that needs to be nurtured and built.

Garrard concludes that if you want to be free you should lean into the uncertainty. He writes, "A significant amount of psychological research has shown us that people find self-determination empowering and motivating. Taking a more skills-powered view of careers might make it more difficult to plot out our future in an obvious way, which some people will find uncomfortable. However, the opportunity for greater freedom and experimentation in our work and in our lives is an idea worth leaning into. If organizations, communities and governments can find ways to help individuals identify and respond to the right signals about skills at the right time, it's possible that it could be a win-win for everyone."[8]

Final Words

The skills-powered organization might seem daunting, but it is here to stay. Many organizations have started to realize the promise of exponentially greater agility, resilience, inclusivity, and productivity that comes from embarking on this journey. Take the opportunity to understand and experiment with being a skills-powered organization now, and you will be better prepared to face the vital challenges of the future. We hope our ideas, experiences, examples, and guidance are useful resources on your journey.

Acknowledgments

We are most grateful for the support of our many colleagues who inspired and challenged us in the writing of this book, including those at Mercer and Standard Chartered. We are particularly grateful to Mercer colleagues Ilya Bonic, Paul Habgood, Lewis Garrard, Molly Ladd, Lisa Enriquez, and Darcy Jacobsen and Standard Chartered colleagues Divya Handa and Catherine Woods for their support and contributions. We also greatly appreciate Karen Kocher's contributions in sharing the Microsoft story.

We are thankful for the generous counsel and insights of our manuscript reviewers and the great team at the MIT Press. We are particularly grateful for the incredible patience and support from our editor Catherine Woods, whose coaching and insights made this book so much better.

Last, but by no means least, we are eternally grateful for the support and encouragement of our spouses, Maureen Jesuthasan and Abhinav Sinha, without whom this book would never have been possible.

Notes

Introduction

1. "Computer and Information Technology Occupations," US Bureau of Labor Statistics, May 14, 2021, https://www.bls.gov/ooh/computer-and-information-technology/home.htm.

2. Ginni Rometty, "We Need to Fill 'New Collar' Jobs That Employers Demand: IBM's Rometty," *USA Today*, December 13, 2016, https://www.usatoday.com/story/tech/columnist/2016/12/13/we-need-fill-new-collar-jobs-employers-demand-ibms-rometty/95382248/.

3. "Make It," CNBC, March 2, 2016, https://www.cnbc.com/make-it/.

4. "IBM News Room," accessed June 26, 2021, https://www-03.ibm.com/press/us/en/pressrelease/52552.wss.

5. Sue Cantrell, Robin Jones, Michael Griffiths, and Julie Hiipakka, "The Skills-Powered Organization: A New Operating Model for Work and the Workforce," Deloitte, September 8, 2022, https://www2.deloitte.com/us/en/insights/topics/talent/organizational-skill-based-hiring.html.

6. Accenture, *Future Skills Pilot Report: Thinking outside the Box to Reimagine Talent Mobility* (Dublin: Accenture, 2021), https://www.accenture.com/us-en/case-studies/consulting/future-skills-pilot-report.

7. John W. Boudreau and Pete Ramstad, *Beyond HR: The New Science of Human Capital* (Boston, MA: Harvard Business School Press, 2007).

8. John Boudreau, Ravin Jesuthasan, and David Creelman, *Lead the Work: Navigating a World Beyond Employment* (Hoboken, NJ: John Wiley & Sons, 2015).

9. Ravin Jesuthasan and John W. Boudreau, *Reinventing Jobs: A 4-Step Approach for Applying Automation to Work* (Boston, MA: Harvard Business Review Press, 2018).

10. Ravin Jesuthasan and John W. Boudreau, *Work without Jobs: How to Reboot Your Organization's Work Operating Systems* (Cambridge, MA: MIT Press, 2022).

11. Frederick Winslow Taylor, *Principles of Scientific Management* (New York: Harper & Brothers, 1911).

12. David H. Autor, Lawrence F. Katz, and Melissa S. Kearney, "The Polarization of the US Labor Market," *American Economic Review* 96, no. 2: 189–194.

13. World Economic Forum, *Future of Jobs Report 2023* (Cologny/Geneva: World Economic Forum, 2023), https://www3.weforum.org/docs/WEF_Future_of_Jobs_2023 .pdf.

14. World Economic Forum, "Putting Skills First: A Framework for Action," white paper, May 2023, https://www.weforum.org/publications/putting-skills-first-a-frame work-for-action/.

Chapter 1

1. World Economic Forum, *Future of Jobs Report 2023* (Cologny/Geneva: World Economic Forum, 2023), https://www3.weforum.org/docs/WEF_Future_of_Jobs_2023 .pdf.

2. LinkedIn, *Skills-First: Reimagining the Labor Market and Breaking Down Barriers* (San Francisco, CA: LinkedIn, 2023). https://economicgraph.linkedin.com/content/dam /me/economicgraph/en-us/PDF/skills-first-report-2023.pdf.

3. McKinsey, "American Opportunity Survey," April 2022, https://www.mckinsey .com/featured-insights/sustainable-inclusive-growth/future-of-america/american -opportunity-survey.

4. World Economic Forum, "Putting Skills First: A Framework for Action," white paper, May 2023, https://www.weforum.org/publications/putting-skills-first-a-fram ework-for-action/.

5. "Governance and Guidance for Growth through Human Capability (G3HC)," G3 Human Capability, accessed July 1, 2023, https://www.g3humancapability.com/.

6. Nik Dawson et al., *How Skills Are Disrupting Work: The Transformational Power of Fast-Growing, In-Demand Skills* (Philadelphia, PA: Burning Glass Institute, 2022), https://www.burningglassinstitute.org/research/how-skills-are-disrupting-work.

7. Burning Glass Institute and Coursera, *2023 Skills Compass Report* (Philadelphia, PA: Burning Glass Institute, 2023), https://www.burningglassinstitute.org/research /2023-skills-compass-report.

8. Ravin Jesuthasan and John W. Boudreau, *Reinventing Jobs: A 4-Step Approach for Applying Automation to Work* (Boston, MA: Harvard Business Review Press, 2018).

9. Ravin Jesuthasan and John W. Boudreau, *Work without Jobs: How to Reboot Your Organization's Work Operating Systems* (Cambridge, MA: MIT Press, 2022).

10. Tera Allas and Bill Schaninger, "The Boss Factor: Making the World a Better Place through Workplace Relationships," McKinsey, September 22, 2020, https://www.mckinsey.com/business-functions/organization/our-insights/the-boss-factor-making-the-world-a-better-place-through-workplace-relationships.

11. "Leadership Agreement," accessed March 19, 2024, https://av.sc.com/corp-en/content/docs/Final_Leadership_Agreement_Visual.pdf.

Chapter 2

1. Arthur Yeung and Dave Ulrich, *Reinventing the Organization: How Companies Can Deliver Radically Greater Value in Fast-Changing Markets* (Boston, MA: Harvard Business Review Press, 2019).

2. Ravin Jesuthasan and John W. Boudreau, *Work without Jobs: How to Reboot Your Organization's Work Operating Systems* (Cambridge, MA: MIT Press, 2022).

3. Jesuthasan and Boudreau, *Work without Jobs*.

Chapter 3

1. Ravin Jesuthasan and John W. Boudreau, *Work without Jobs: How to Reboot Your Organization's Work Operating Systems* (Cambridge, MA: MIT Press, 2022).

2. Arthur Yeung and Dave Ulrich, *Reinventing the Organization: How Companies Can Deliver Radically Greater Value in Fast-Changing Markets* (Boston, MA: Harvard Business Review Press, 2019).

3. "Holacracy," accessed April 9, 2021, https://www.holacracy.org/.

4. Gary Hamel and Michele Zanini, *Humanocracy: Creating Organizations as Amazing as the People inside Them* (Boston, MA: Harvard Business Review Press, 2020).

5. Adapted from Jesuthasan and Boudreau, *Work without Jobs*.

6. Adi Gaskell, "Covid Saw a Boost in Online Learning among Women," *Forbes*, November 11, 2021, https://www.forbes.com/sites/adigaskell/2021/11/23/covid-saw-a-boost-in-online-learning-among-women/?sh=76901751325f.

7. Tara S. Mohr, "Why Women Don't Apply for Jobs Unless They're 100% Qualified," *Harvard Business Review*, August 25, 2014, https://hbr.org/2014/08/why-women-dont-apply-for-jobs-unless-theyre-100-qualified.

8. Rachel Thomas et al., *Women in the Workplace 2023* (Los Angeles: McKinsey, 2023), https://www.mckinsey.com/featured-insights/diversity-and-inclusion/women-in-the-workplace.

9. "FSSC and PwC Research Shows Re-skilling Saves Businesses up to £49,100 per Employee," January 27, 2022, https://financialservicesskills.org/news/new-partner -research-shows-re-skilling-saves-businesses-up-to-49100-per-employee/.

Chapter 4

1. Gary A. Bolles, *The Next Rules of Work: The Mindset, Skillset and Toolset to Lead Your Organization through Uncertainty* (London: Kogan Page, 2021).

2. Ravin Jesuthasan and John W. Boudreau, *Reinventing Jobs: A 4-Step Approach for Applying Automation to Work* (Boston, MA: Harvard Business Review Press, 2018).

3. John W. Boudreau, *Retooling HR: Using Proven Business Tools to Make Better Decisions about Talent* (Boston, MA: Harvard Business Review Press, 2014); John W. Boudreau and Ravin Jesuthasan, *Transformative HR: How Great Companies Use Evidence-Based Change for Sustainable Advantage* (San Francisco: Jossey-Bass, 2011).

4. John Boudreau, Ravin Jesuthasan, and David Creelman, *Lead the Work: Navigating a World Beyond Employment* (Hoboken, NJ: John Wiley & Sons, 2015).

5. Ravin Jesuthasan, "Metrics for the Future of Work," HR Tech Outlook, accessed April 9, 2021, https://hr-analytics.hrtechoutlook.com/cxoinsights/metrics-for-the -future-of-work-nid-765.html.

6. Mercer, *Building and Sustaining a Thriving Talent Marketplace* (New York: Mercer, 2022).

Chapter 5

1. Microsoft, *2023 Work Trend Index: Annual Report* (Redmond, WA: Microsoft, 2023)

2. Seth Patton, "Introducing Skills in Microsoft Viva, a New AI-Powered Service to Grow and Manage Talent," Microsoft 365 Blog, October 10, 2023, https://www .microsoft.com/en-us/microsoft-365/blog/2023/10/10/introducing-skills-in-microsoft -viva-a-new-ai-powered-service-to-grow-and-manage-talent/.

Chapter 6

1. World Economic Forum, "HR4.0: Shaping People Strategies in the Fourth Industrial Revolution, white paper, December 2019, https://www.weforum.org /publications/hr4-0-shaping-people-strategies-in-the-fourth-industrial-revolution/.

2. Kate Gautier et al., "Research: How Employee Experience Impacts Your Bottom Line," *Harvard Business Review*, March 22, 2022, https://hbr.org/2022/03/research -how-employee-experience-impacts-your-bottom-line.

3. "What Is Employee Engagement and How Do You Improve It?," Gallup, accessed July 1, 2023, https://www.gallup.com/workplace/285674/improve-employee-engage ment-workplace.aspx.

4. Goldman Sachs Global Investment Research, *The Potentially Large Effects of Artificial Intelligence on Economic Growth* (New York: Goldman Sachs, 2023), https://www .key4biz.it/wp-content/uploads/2023/03/Global-Economics-Analyst_-The-Potentially -Large-Effects-of-Artificial-Intelligence-on-Economic-Growth-Briggs_Kodnani.pdf.

5. Paul Daugherty et al., *A New Era of Generative AI for Everyone* (Dublin: Accenture, 2023), https://www.accenture.com/content/dam/accenture/final/accenture-com/docu ment/Accenture-A-New-Era-of-Generative-AI-for-Everyone.pdf.

Chapter 7

1. Arthur Yeung and Dave Ulrich, *Reinventing the Organization: How Companies Can Deliver Radically Greater Value in Fast-Changing Markets* (Boston, MA: Harvard Business Review Press, 2019)..

2. Gary A. Bolles, "The Future of the Organization Is Community," LinkedIn, October 15, 2023, https://www.linkedin.com/pulse/future-organization-community-gary -a-bolles/.

3. Ravin Jesuthasan and George Zarkadakis, "How Will Web3 Impact the Future of Work?," World Economic Forum, July 25, 2022, https://www.weforum.org /agenda/2022/07/web-3-change-the-future-of-work-decentralized-autonomous -organizations/.

4. Opportunity@Work and Accenture, *Reach for the STARs: Realizing the Potential of America's Hidden Talent Pool* (Washington, DC: Opportunity@Work and Accenture, 2020).

5. "About SkillsFuture," SkillsFuture, accessed July 1, 2023, https://www.skillsfuture .gov.sg/aboutskillsfuture.

6. European Commission, "The French Skills Investment Plan," March 2021, https:// ec.europa.eu/social/BlobServlet?docId=23755&langId=en.

7. Service-Public, "Personal Training Account (PTA) of a Private Sector Employee," January 1, 2023, https://www.service-public.fr/particuliers/vosdroits/F10705?lang=en.

Chapter 8

1. Adapted from Lewis Garrard, "Redesigning Your Career Path in a Skills-Driven World," Mercer, accessed September 1, 2023, https://www.mercer.com/insights /talent-and-transformation/skill-based-talent-management/redesigning-your-career -path-in-a-skills-driven-world.

2. Ayelet Fishbach, "In Choosing a Job, Focus on the Fun," *New York Times*, January 13, 2017, https://www.nytimes.com/2017/01/13/jobs/in-choosing-a-job-focus-on-the-fun.html.

3. "Unlock the Power and Potential of your Workforce," Mercer, accessed September 1, 2023, https://www.mercer.com/solutions/transformation/workforce-and-organization-transformation/talent-marketplace/.

4. Anthony Santa Maria, "What Is a Skills Taxonomy and Why Do You Need It?," LinkedIn Talent Blog, May 29, 2023, https://www.linkedin.com/business/talent/blog/learning-and-development/what-is-a-skills-taxonomy-and-why-do-you-need-it.

5. World Economic Forum, *Building a Common Language for Skills at Work: A Global Taxonomy* (Cologny/Geneva: World Economic Forum, 2021), https://www.weforum.org/reports/building-a-common-language-for-skills-at-work-a-global-taxonomy.

6. Lewis Garrad, "What Are the Skills Needed to Create a Culture of Lifelong Learning?," myHRfuture, October 1, 2020, https://www.myhrfuture.com/blog/2020/9/30/what-are-the-skills-needed-to-create-a-culture-of-lifelong-learning.

7. Brian R. Little, "Personality Psychology: Havings, Doings, and Beings in Context," October 24, 2011, http://www.brianrlittle.com/Topics/research/personal-projects-analysis/?doing_wp_cron=1689217341.4271740913391113281250.

8. Garrard, "Redesigning Your Career Path in a Skills-Driven World." For more on self-determination, see Center for Self-Determination Theory, "Theory," accessed September 1, 2023, https://selfdeterminationtheory.org/theory/.

Index